Second Edition

GREAT JOBS

FOR

Geology Majors

Blythe Camenson

New York Chicago San Francisco Lisbon London Madrid Mexico City
Milan New Delhi San Juan Seoul Singapore Sydney Toronto

Library of Congress Cataloging-in-Publication Data

Camenson, Blythe.
    Great jobs for geology majors / Blythe Camenson. — 2nd ed.
        p.   cm.
    Includes index.
    ISBN 0-07-146775-0 (pbk. : acid-free paper)
    1. Geology—Vocational guidance.   I. Title.

   QE34.C36   2007
   550′.23—dc22   2006046190

1 2 3 4 5 6 7 8 9 10 11 12 13 14 15 16 17 18 19 20 21   DOC/DOC 0 9 8 7 6

ISBN-13: 978-0-07-146775-9
ISBN-10:   0-07-146775-0

McGraw-Hill books are available at special quantity discounts to use as premiums and sales promotions, or for use in corporate training programs. For more information, please write to the Director of Special Sales, Professional Publishing, McGraw-Hill, Two Penn Plaza, New York, NY 10121-2298. Or contact your local bookstore.

This book is printed on acid-free paper.

Contents

Introduction

Geology: Unearthing Your Future

What can you do with a degree in geology? The answer is almost anything you choose. A geology degree will prepare you for a wide range of careers. Career options include—but are not limited to—research for an academic institution, a government agency, or a private firm; teaching at a college or university or even in a primary or secondary school; environmental and engineering consulting; pollution remediation; environmental law and public policy; or government work in the U.S. Foreign Service, the Air Force, NASA, the National Park Service, or the Peace Corps. But that's not all. Geology opens doors in outdoor education, resource exploration, natural hazard prediction, rural and urban planning, computer systems and support— even medical school!

Although options are available to geologists with bachelor's degrees, this is an area in which a graduate degree is recommended or required to enter many career paths. In fact, for many positions, a doctoral degree is needed to show you have the credentials to perform the work. No matter what degree you hold and career path you pursue, as a geologist, you will be a lifetime-learner.

The Future of Geology

Scientists report that our world has entered a period of environmental crisis. Our very success has become a threat to humanity. Our population continues to explode; our environment continues to be negatively affected by human ignorance and greed. As a result, traditional career paths in the earth sciences shifted as world governments, industries, and social structures react to the many forms of global change.

Global change is not a new idea to geoscientists; the nature of the work means they are aware of the huge modifications constantly being made to our planet. Now geoscientists have begun—and will continue—to interact with other scientists and with businesses and governments even more than they have in the past. The potential problems we face require geoscientific expertise, with cooperation among chemists, physicists, mathematicians, biologists, anthropologists, and engineers. Those responsible for effecting change and resolving the problems will most likely act on the advice of frontline geoscientists.

Geology is an area in which advancing technologies are helping those in the field better understand their area of study. Laboratory equipment refines the identification and analysis process. A variety of software programs are available to help geologists do everything—analyze data, visualize images, predict erosion, map plate tectonics, and simulate the impact of volcanic activity. As in most areas of scientific study and research, new technologies will continue to be invented and refined to further the field of geology.

The Role of the Geologist

Geoscientists wear many different hats, and the roles they play are crucial to the survival of the planet. Geologists are responsible for locating mineral deposits and energy resources for the future. They decide the sources and management of water supplies. They are involved in ensuring that waste products are stored or disposed of safely, with the smallest possible threat to ecosystems. They contribute to the protection of the planet and its resources by their studies of the environment. They help determine the cost and location of new structures. They consider environmental hazards when planning cities, highways, and pipelines. They record the creation and movements of the continents. They observe the movement of glaciers and the rise and fall of sea levels. They contribute to the understanding and prediction of natural hazards and disasters, such as earthquakes, landslides, volcanic eruptions, floods, and droughts. They observe and record changes in the diversity of life. No matter what your particular area of interest, if you have a desire to understand the structure of the earth, you'll find an exciting career path to pursue in geology.

The Road Ahead

In Part One of this book, you will learn many valuable tips about the job search, including how to construct a resume and how to master the intimidating interview process. In Part Two, you will explore a variety of career paths. Some are open to any geology major; some are more defined and require training in specific subfields; still others require further formal education or training such as master's degrees and, more often, doctorates.

Chapter 9 will give you a broad overview of the various paths and the training and preparation you'll need. The remaining chapters will help you narrow those paths. Once you've found the path you want to follow, you'll realize how important your geology degree is in reaching your ultimate destination. As you'll soon discover, your geology degree will lead to a rewarding career, no matter which path you ultimately choose.

PART ONE

THE JOB SEARCH

1

The Self-Assessment

Self-assessment is the process by which you begin to acknowledge your own particular blend of education, experiences, values, needs, and goals. It provides the foundation for career planning and the entire job search process. Self-assessment involves looking inward and asking yourself what can sometimes prove to be difficult questions. This self-examination should lead to an intimate understanding of your personal traits and values, consumption patterns and economic needs, longer-term goals, skill base, preferred skills, and underdeveloped skills.

You come to the self-assessment process knowing yourself well in some of these areas, but you may still be uncertain about other aspects. You may be well aware of your consumption patterns, but have you spent much time specifically identifying your longer-term goals or your personal values as they relate to work? No matter what level of self-assessment you have undertaken to date, it is now time to clarify all of these issues and questions as they relate to the job search.

The knowledge you gain in the self-assessment process will guide the rest of your job search. In this book, you will learn about all of the following tasks:

- Writing résumés and cover letters
- Researching careers and networking
- Interviewing and job offer considerations

In each of these steps, you will rely on and often return to the understanding gained through your self-assessment. Any individual seeking employment must be able and willing to express these facets of his or her personality

3

to recruiters and interviewers throughout the job search. This communication allows you to show the world who you are so that together with employers you can determine whether there will be a workable match with a given job or career path.

How to Conduct a Self-Assessment

The self-assessment process goes on naturally all the time. People ask you to clarify what you mean, you make a purchasing decision, or you begin a new relationship. You react to the world and the world reacts to you. How you understand these interactions and any changes you might make because of them are part of the natural process of self-discovery. There is, however, a more comprehensive and efficient way to approach self-assessment with regard to employment.

Because self-assessment can become a complex exercise, we have distilled it into a seven-step process that provides an effective basis for undertaking a job search. The seven steps include the following:

1. Understanding your personal traits
2. Identifying your personal values
3. Calculating your economic needs
4. Exploring your longer-term goals
5. Enumerating your skill base
6. Recognizing your preferred skills
7. Assessing skills needing further development

As you work through your self-assessment, you might want to create a worksheet similar to the one shown in Exhibit 1.1, starting on the following page. Or you might want to keep a journal of the thoughts you have as you undergo this process. There will be many opportunities to revise your self-assessment as you start down the path of seeking a career.

Step 1   Understand Your Personal Traits
Each person has a unique personality that he or she brings to the job search process. Gaining a better understanding of your personal traits can help you evaluate job and career choices. Identifying these traits and then finding employment that allows you to draw on at least some of them can create a rewarding and fulfilling work experience. If potential employment doesn't allow you to use these preferred traits, it is important to decide whether you

Exhibit 1.1
SELF-ASSESSMENT WORKSHEET

Step 1. Understand Your Personal Traits

The personal traits that describe me are
(Include all of the words that describe you.)
The ten personal traits that most accurately describe me are
(List these ten traits.)

Step 2. Identify Your Personal Values

Working conditions that are important to me include
(List working conditions that would have to exist for you to accept a position.)
The values that go along with my working conditions are
(Write down the values that correspond to each working condition.)
Some additional values I've decided to include are
(List those values you identify as you conduct this job search.)

Step 3. Calculate Your Economic Needs

My estimated minimum annual salary requirement is
(Write the salary you have calculated based on your budget.)
Starting salaries for the positions I'm considering are
(List the name of each job you are considering and the associated starting salary.)

Step 4. Explore Your Longer-Term Goals

My thoughts on longer-term goals right now are
(Jot down some of your longer-term goals as you know them right now.)

Step 5. Enumerate Your Skill Base

The general skills I possess are
(List the skills that underlie tasks you are able to complete.)
The specific skills I possess are
(List more technical or specific skills that you possess, and indicate your level of expertise.)
General and specific skills that I want to promote to employers for the jobs I'm considering are
(List general and specific skills for each type of job you are considering.)

continued

Step 6. Recognize Your Preferred Skills

Skills that I would like to use on the job include

(List skills that you hope to use on the job, and indicate how often you'd like to use them.)

Step 7. Assess Skills Needing Further Development

Some skills that I'll need to acquire for the jobs I'm considering include

(Write down skills listed in job advertisements or job descriptions that you don't currently possess.)

I believe I can build these skills by

(Describe how you plan to acquire these skills.)

can find other ways to express them or whether you would be better off not considering this type of job. Interests and hobbies pursued outside of work hours can be one way to use personal traits you don't have an opportunity to draw on in your work. For example, if you consider yourself an outgoing person and the kinds of jobs you are examining allow little contact with other people, you may be able to achieve the level of interaction that is comfortable for you outside of your work setting. If such a compromise seems impractical or otherwise unsatisfactory, you probably should explore only jobs that provide the interaction you want and need on the job.

Many young adults who are not very confident about their employability will downplay their need for income. They will say, "Money is not all that important if I love my work." But if you begin to document exactly what you need for housing, transportation, insurance, clothing, food, and utilities, you will begin to understand that some jobs cannot meet your financial needs and it doesn't matter how wonderful the job is. If you have to worry each payday about bills and other financial obligations, you won't be very effective on the job. Begin now to be honest with yourself about your needs.

Begin the self-assessment process by creating an inventory of your personal traits. Make a list of as many words as possible to describe yourself. Words like *accurate, creative, future-oriented, relaxed,* or *structured* are just a few examples. In addition, you might ask people who know you well how they might describe you.

Focus on Selected Personal Traits. Of all the traits you identified, select the ten you believe most accurately describe you. Keep track of these ten traits.

Consider Your Personal Traits in the Job Search Process. As you begin exploring jobs and careers, watch for matches between your personal traits and the job descriptions you read. Some jobs will require many personal traits you know you possess, and others will not seem to match those traits.

A researcher's work, for example, requires an attention to detail, self-discipline, motivation, curiosity, and observation. Researchers often work on the same project for an extended period of time and they tend to work alone or in a small group, with limited opportunities to interact with others. Professors, on the other hand, must interact regularly with students and colleagues to carry out their teaching program. Educators need strong interpersonal and verbal skills, imagination, and a good sense of humor. They must enjoy being in front of groups and must become skilled at presenting information using a variety of methods to appeal to various learning styles.

Your ability to respond to changing conditions, your decision-making ability, productivity, creativity, and verbal skills all have a bearing on your success in and enjoyment of your work life. To better guarantee success, be sure to take the time needed to understand these traits in yourself.

Step 2   Identify Your Personal Values

Your personal values affect every aspect of your life, including employment, and they develop and change as you move through life. Values can be defined as principles that we hold in high regard, qualities that are important and desirable to us. Some values aren't ordinarily connected to work (love, beauty, color, light, relationships, family, or religion), and others are (autonomy, cooperation, effectiveness, achievement, knowledge, and security). Our values determine, in part, the level of satisfaction we feel in a particular job.

Define Acceptable Working Conditions. One facet of employment is the set of working conditions that must exist for someone to consider taking a job.

Each of us would probably create a unique list of acceptable working conditions, but items that might be included on many people's lists are the amount of money you would need to be paid, how far you are willing to drive or travel, the amount of freedom you want in determining your own schedule, whether you would be working with people or data or things, and the types of tasks you would be willing to do. Your conditions might include statements of working conditions you will *not* accept; for example, you might not be willing to work at night or on weekends or holidays.

If you were offered a job tomorrow, what conditions would have to exist for you to realistically consider accepting the position? Take some time and make a list of these conditions.

Realize Associated Values. Your list of working conditions can be used to create an inventory of your values relating to jobs and careers you are exploring. For example, if one of your conditions stated that you wanted to earn at least $30,000 per year, the associated value would be financial gain. If another condition was that you wanted to work with a friendly group of people, the value that went along with that might be belonging or interaction with people.

Relate Your Values to the World of Work. As you read the job descriptions you come across either in this book, in newspapers and magazines, or online, think about the values associated with each position.

For example, the environmental earth science professional may consult on the clean-up of environmental hazards or toxins or predict natural disasters and how best to limit damage to property and loss of life. Associated values include a sense of community, environmental protection and preservation, veracity (truthfulness), and beneficence (doing good).

At least some of the associated values in the field you're exploring should match those you extracted from your list of working conditions. Take a second look at any values that don't match up. How important are they to you? What will happen if they are not satisfied on the job? Can you incorporate those personal values elsewhere? Your answers need to be brutally honest. As you continue your exploration, be sure to add to your list any additional values that occur to you.

Step 3 Calculate Your Economic Needs

Each of us grew up in an environment that provided for certain basic needs, such as food and shelter, and, to varying degrees, other needs that we now consider basic, such as cable television, e-mail, or an automobile. Needs such as privacy, space, and quiet, which at first glance may not appear to be monetary needs, may add to housing expenses and so should be considered as you examine your economic needs. For example, if you place a high value on a large, open living space for yourself, it would be difficult to satisfy that need without an associated high housing cost, especially in a densely populated city environment.

As you prepare to move into the world of work and become responsible for meeting your own basic needs, it is important to consider the salary you will need to be able to afford a satisfying standard of living. The three-step process outlined here will help you plan a budget, which in turn will allow you to evaluate the various career choices and geographic locations you are considering. The steps include (1) develop a realistic budget, (2) examine starting salaries, and (3) use a cost-of-living index.

Develop a Realistic Budget. Each of us has certain expectations for the kind of lifestyle we want to maintain. To begin the process of defining your economic needs, it will be helpful to determine what you expect to spend on routine monthly expenses. These expenses include housing, food, transportation, entertainment, utilities, loan repayments, and revolving charge accounts. You may not currently spend anything for certain items, but you probably will have to once you begin supporting yourself. As you develop this budget, be generous in your estimates, but keep in mind any items that could be reduced or eliminated. If you are not sure about the cost of a certain item, talk with family or friends who would be able to give you a realistic estimate.

If this is new or difficult for you, start to keep a log of expenses right now. You may be surprised at how much you actually spend each month for food or stamps or magazines. Household expenses and personal grooming items can often loom very large in a budget, as can auto repairs or home maintenance.

Income taxes must also be taken into consideration when examining salary requirements. State and local taxes vary, so it is difficult to calculate exactly the effect of taxes on the amount of income you need to generate. To roughly estimate the gross income necessary to generate your minimum annual salary requirement, multiply the minimum salary you have calculated by a factor of 1.35. The resulting figure will be an approximation of what your gross income would need to be, given your estimated expenses.

Examine Starting Salaries. Starting salaries for each of the career tracks are provided throughout this book. These salary figures can be used in conjunction with the cost-of-living index (discussed in the next section) to determine whether you would be able to meet your basic economic needs in a given geographic location.

Use a Cost-of-Living Index. If you are thinking about trying to get a job in a geographic region other than the one where you now live, understanding differences in the cost of living will help you come to a more informed decision about making a move. By using a cost-of-living index, you can compare salaries offered and the cost of living in different locations with what you know about the salaries offered and the cost of living in your present location.

Many variables are used to calculate the cost-of-living index. Often included are housing, groceries, utilities, transportation, health care, clothing, and entertainment expenses. Right now you do not need to worry about the details associated with calculating a given index. The main purpose of this exercise is to help you understand that pay ranges for entry-level positions may not vary greatly, but the cost of living in different locations *can* vary tremendously.

Suppose you live in Juneau, Alaska, and you are interested in working as a geoscientist for the state government. The U.S. Department of Labor's Bureau of Labor Statistics (bls.gov) reports that the approximate annual salary for a geoscientist position might be about $45,000. Perhaps the cold weather is starting to get to you and you're considering moving to Honolulu, Hawaii, or San Diego, California. You know you can live on $45,000 in Juneau, but you want to be able to equal that salary in other locations you're considering. How much will you need to earn in those locations to do this? Figuring the cost of living for each city will show you.

In any cost-of-living index, the number 100 represents the national average cost of living, and each city is assigned an index number based on current prices in that city for the items included in the index (housing, food, salary, etc.). As you can imagine, these indices are constantly changing. In this example, Juneau's index is 100.0, Honolulu's is 198.0, and San Diego's is 169.5. In other words, it costs nearly twice as much to live in Hawaii and about one and a half times as much to live in California as it does to live in Alaska. The following table shows you how much you would have to earn in each of these cities to maintain the same style of living as you would have in Alaska on a $45,000 salary.

JOB: GEOSCIENTIST

City	Index	Equivalent Salary
Honolulu	198.0	
		$\dfrac{198.0}{100.0} \times \$45,000 = \$89,100$ in Honolulu
Juneau	100.0	
San Diego	169.5	
		$\dfrac{169.5}{100.0} \times \$45,000 = \$76,275$ in San Diego
Juneau	100.0	

This means that you'll need to make significantly more in both warmer cities to maintain your current standard of living. On the other hand, just think of the money you'll save on not having to pay heating costs and for winter clothes!

If you have an aversion to math, there are a variety of salary converters online that will do the work for you. Simply type "salary conversion" or "salary calculator" into a search engine and you'll find plenty of free choices.

You can work through a similar exercise for any type of job you are considering and for many locations when current salary information is available. It will be worth your time to undertake this analysis if you are seriously considering a relocation. By doing so you will be able to make an informed choice.

Step 4 Explore Your Longer-Term Goals

There is no question that when we first begin working, our goals are to use our skills and education in a job that will reward us with employment, income, and status relative to the preparation we brought with us to this position. If we are not being paid as much as we feel we should for our level of education or if job demands don't provide the intellectual stimulation we had hoped for, we experience unhappiness and as a result often seek other employment.

Most jobs we consider "good" are those that fulfill our basic "lower-level" needs of security, food, clothing, shelter, income, and productive work. But even when our basic needs are met and our jobs are secure and productive, we as individuals are constantly changing. As we change, the demands and expectations we place on our jobs may change. Fortunately, some jobs grow and change with us, and this explains why some people are happy throughout many years in a job.

But more often people are bigger than the jobs they fill. We have more goals and needs than any job could satisfy. These are "higher-level" needs of self-esteem, companionship, affection, and an increasing desire to feel we are employing ourselves in the most effective way possible. Not all of these higher-level needs can be met through employment, but for as long as we are employed, we increasingly demand that our jobs play their part in moving us along the path to fulfillment.

Another obvious but important fact is that we change as we mature. Although our jobs also have the potential for change, they may not change as frequently or as markedly as we do. There are increasingly fewer one-job, one-employer careers; we must think about a work future that may involve voluntary or forced moves from employer to employer. Because of that very real possibility, we need to take advantage of the opportunities in each position we hold. Acquiring the skills and competencies associated with each position will keep us viable and attractive as employees. This is particularly true in a job market that not only is technology/computer dependent, but also is populated with more and more small, self-transforming organizations rather than the large, seemingly stable organizations of the past.

If you are considering a position as a geologist working for an oil company, you would gain a better perspective on this career if you talked to an entry-level technician, a more experienced assistant geologist, and finally a director or department head who has a considerable work history in the oil industry. Ask these persons to grant you an informational interview and come prepared with questions about how they obtained their current positions.

Step 5   Enumerate Your Skill Base

In terms of the job search, skills can be thought of as capabilities that can be developed in school, at work, or by volunteering and then used in specific job settings. Many studies have documented the kinds of skills that employers seek in entry-level applicants. For example, some of the most desired skills for individuals interested in the teaching profession are the ability to interact effectively with students one-on-one, to manage a classroom, to adapt to varying situations as necessary, and to get involved in school activities. Business employers have also identified important qualities, including enthusiasm for the employer's product or service, a businesslike mind, the ability to follow written or oral instructions, the ability to demonstrate self-control, the confidence to suggest new ideas, the ability to communicate with all members of a group, an awareness of cultural differences, and loyalty, to name just a few. You will find that many of these skills are also in the repertoire of qualities demanded in your college major.

To be successful in obtaining any given job, you must be able to demonstrate that you possess a certain mix of skills that will allow you to carry out the duties required by that job. This skill mix will vary a great deal from job to job; to determine the skills necessary for the jobs you are seeking, you can read job advertisements or more generic job descriptions, such as those found later in this book. If you want to be effective in the job search, you must directly show employers that you possess the skills needed to be successful in filling the position. These skills will initially be described on your résumé and then discussed again during the interview process.

Skills are either general or specific. To develop a list of skills relevant to employers, you must first identify the general skills you possess, then list specific skills you have to offer, and, finally, examine which of these skills employers are seeking.

Identify Your General Skills. Because you possess or will possess a college degree, employers will assume that you can read and write, perform certain basic computations, think critically, and communicate effectively. Employers will want to see that you have acquired these skills, and they will want to know which additional general skills you possess.

One way to begin identifying skills is to write an experiential diary. An experiential diary lists all the tasks you were responsible for completing for each job you've held and then outlines the skills required to do those tasks. You may list several skills for any given task. This diary allows you to distinguish between the tasks you performed and the underlying skills required to complete those tasks. Here's an example:

Tasks	Skills
Answering telephone	Effective use of language, clear diction, ability to direct inquiries, ability to solve problems
Waiting on tables	Poise under conditions of time and pressure, speed, accuracy, good memory, simultaneous completion of tasks, sales skills

For each job or experience you have participated in, develop a worksheet based on the example shown here. On a résumé, you may want to describe these skills rather than simply listing tasks. Skills are easier for the employer to appreciate, especially when your experience is very different from the employment you are seeking. In addition to helping you identify general skills, this experiential diary will prepare you to speak more effectively in an interview about the qualifications you possess.

Identify Your Specific Skills. It may be easier to identify your specific skills because you can definitely say whether you can speak other languages, program a computer, draft a map or diagram, or edit a document using appropriate symbols and terminology.

Using your experiential diary, identify the points in your history where you learned how to do something very specific, and decide whether you have a beginning, intermediate, or advanced knowledge of how to use that particular skill. Right now, be sure to list *every* specific skill you have, and don't consider whether you like using the skill. Write down a list of specific skills you have acquired and the level of competence you possess—beginning, intermediate, or advanced.

Relate Your Skills to Employers. You probably have thought about a couple of different jobs you might be interested in obtaining, and one way to begin relating the general and specific skills you possess to a potential employer's needs is to read actual advertisements for these types of positions (see Part Two for resources listing actual job openings).

Let's say you're interested in a career as a college geology professor. A typical job listing might read, "Requires minimum Ph.D., five years teaching experience, organizational and interpersonal skills, imagination, drive, and the ability to work with students from a variety of backgrounds." If you used any of a number of general sources of information that describe the job of college geology professor, you would find additional information about general expectations for college professors. For example, professors develop lesson plans, evaluate performance, work with other faculty, publish articles in professional journals, and have an area of specialization within the general field of geology.

While conducting research on job expectations for college professors, build a comprehensive list of required skills. Exploring advertisements for descriptions of several types of related positions will reveal an important core of skills necessary for obtaining the type of work you're interested in. Include both general and specific skills. The following is a sample list of skills you would need to be successful as a college professor.

JOB: COLLEGE GEOLOGY PROFESSOR

General Skills	Specific Skills
Collect data	Research plate tectonics
Disseminate information	Lecture to students and peers
Work well with others	Collaborate with faculty
Exhibit creativity	Engage students in discussion
Evaluate performance	Construct exams and grade papers
Possess organizational skills	Design courses that elicit positive student evaluations

---

Now, on a separate sheet of paper, practice by generating a comprehensive list of skills required for at least one job you are considering. The list of general skills for a given career path will be valuable for any number of jobs because these are more universal skills. In this case, evaluating performance is a required skill for both college professors and researchers supervising interns. In addition, many of the specific skills will also be transferable to other types of positions.

Step 6   Recognize Your Preferred Skills

In the previous section you developed a comprehensive list of skills that relate to particular career paths that are of interest to you. You can now relate these to skills that you prefer to use. We all use a wide range of skills (some researchers say individuals have a repertoire of about five hundred skills), but we may not particularly be interested in using all of them in our work. There may be some skills that come to us more naturally or that we use successfully time and time again and that we want to continue to use; these are best described as our preferred skills. For this exercise use the list of skills that you created for the previous section, and decide which of them you are *most interested in using* in future work and how often you would like to use them.

You might be interested in using some skills only occasionally, while others you would like to use more regularly. You probably also have skills that you hope you can use constantly.

As you examine job announcements, look for matches between this list of preferred skills and the qualifications described in the advertisements. These skills should be highlighted on your résumé and discussed in job interviews.

Step 7   Assess Skills Needing Further Development

Previously you compiled a list of general and specific skills required for given positions. You already possess some of these skills; those that remain to be developed are your underdeveloped skills.

If you are just beginning the job search, there may be gaps between the qualifications required for some of the jobs you're considering and the skills you possess. The thought of having to admit to and talk about these underdeveloped skills, especially in a job interview, is a frightening one. One way to put a healthy perspective on this subject is to target and relate your exploration of underdeveloped skills to the types of positions you are seeking. Recognizing these shortcomings and planning to overcome them with either on-the-job training or additional formal education can be a positive way to address the concept of underdeveloped skills.

On your worksheet or in your journal, make a list of up to five general or specific skills required for the positions you're interested in that you *don't currently possess*. For each item list an idea you have for specific action you could take to acquire that skill. Do some brainstorming to come up with possible actions. If you have a hard time generating ideas, talk to people currently working in this type of position, professionals in your college career services office, trusted friends, family members, or members of related professional associations.

In the chapter on interviewing, we will discuss in detail how to effectively address questions about underdeveloped skills. Generally speaking, though, employers want genuine answers to these types of questions. They want you to reveal "the real you," and they also want to see how you answer difficult questions. In taking the positive, targeted approach discussed previously, you show the employer that you are willing to continue to learn and that you have a plan for strengthening your job qualifications.

Use Your Self-Assessment

Exploring entry-level career options can be an exciting experience if you have good resources available and will take the time to use them. Can you effectively complete the following tasks?

1. Understand your personality traits and relate them to career choices
2. Define your personal values
3. Determine your economic needs
4. Explore longer-term goals
5. Understand your skill base
6. Recognize your preferred skills
7. Express a willingness to improve on your underdeveloped skills

If so, then you can more meaningfully participate in the job search process by writing a more effective résumé, finding job titles that represent work you are interested in doing, locating job sites that will provide the opportunity for you to use your strengths and skills, networking in an informed way, participating in focused interviews, getting the most out of follow-up contacts, and evaluating job offers to find those that create a good match between you and the employer. The remaining chapters in Part One guide you through these next steps in the job search process. For many job seekers, this process can take anywhere from three months to a year to implement. The time you will need to put into your job search will depend on the type of job you want and the geographic location where you'd like to work. Think of your effort as a job in itself, requiring you to set aside time each week to complete the needed work. Carefully undertaken efforts may reduce the time you need for your job search.

2

The Résumé and Cover Letter

The task of writing a résumé may seem overwhelming if you are unfamiliar with this type of document, but there are some easily understood techniques that can and should be used. This section was written to help you understand the purpose of the résumé, the different types of formats available, and how to write the sections that contain information traditionally found on a résumé. We will present examples and explanations that address questions frequently posed by people writing their first résumé or updating an old one.

Even within the formats and suggestions given, however, there are infinite variations. True, most follow one of the outlines suggested, but you should feel free to adjust the résumé to suit your needs and make it expressive of your life and experience.

Why Write a Résumé?

The purpose of a résumé is to convince an employer that you should be interviewed. Whether you're mailing, faxing, or e-mailing this document, you'll want to present enough information to show that you can make an immediate and valuable contribution to an organization. A résumé is not an in-depth historical or legal document; later in the job search process you may be asked to document your entire work history on an application form and attest to its validity. The résumé should, instead, highlight relevant information pertaining directly to the organization that will receive the document or to the type of position you are seeking.

We will discuss the chronological and digital résumés in detail here. Functional and targeted résumés, which are used much less often, are briefly discussed. The reasons for using one type of résumé over another and the typical format for each are addressed in the following sections.

The Chronological Résumé

The chronological résumé is the most common of the various résumé formats and therefore the format that employers are most used to receiving. This type of résumé is easy to read and understand because it details the chronological progression of jobs you have held. (See Exhibit 2.1.) It begins with your most recent employment and works back in time. If you have a solid work history or have experience that provided growth and development in your duties and responsibilities, a chronological résumé will highlight these achievements. The typical elements of a chronological résumé include the heading, a career objective, educational background, employment experience, activities, and references.

The Heading
The heading consists of your name, address, telephone number, and other means of contact. This may include a fax number, e-mail address, and your home-page address. If you are using a shared e-mail account or a parent's business fax, be sure to let others who use these systems know that you may receive important professional correspondence via these systems. You wouldn't want to miss a vital e-mail or fax! Likewise, if your résumé directs readers to a personal home page on the Web, be certain it's a professional personal home page designed to be viewed and appreciated by a prospective employer. This may mean making substantial changes in the home page you currently mount on the Web.

The Objective
Without a doubt the objective statement is the most challenging part of the résumé for most writers. Even for individuals who have decided on a career path, it can be difficult to encapsulate all they want to say in one or two brief sentences. For job seekers who are unfocused or unclear about their intentions, trying to write this section can inhibit the entire résumé writing process.

Keep the objective as short as possible and no longer than two short sentences.

Exhibit 2.1
CHRONOLOGICAL RÉSUMÉ

RENEE BROWN
3228 N. Seminary Ave.
Chicago, IL 60647
(773) 555-0643
rbrown@xxx.com

OBJECTIVE

Motivated, reliable, and highly organized individual seeking an entry-level position in environmental research. Looking to put my education and training to work in the field, assisting a team of individuals in protecting and preserving the Earth's valuable natural resources.

EDUCATION

University of Chicago—Chicago, IL, Dec. 2002–Dec. 2006
B.S. Environmental Earth Resources
Major GPA: 4.0
Sigma Theta Tau Geological Honors Society member

RELEVANT COURSES

- Advanced Geographic Information Systems
- Remote Sensing Technology
- Seismic Geology
- Preparation of Environmental Impact Statements
- Map Interpretation
- Geomorphology
- Environmental Geology
- Petroleum Geology
- Structural Geology
- Hydrology and Soils

EXPERIENCE

University of Chicago, Earth Science Department—Chicago, IL, Oct. 2003–Nov. 2006

continued

- Department Head Assistant
- Kept schedules, filed papers, assisted with manuscript preparation
- Attended lectures and research symposiums in support capacity

City of Chicago Environmental Quality Division—Chicago, IL, March 2003–June 2005
- Volunteer
- Organized database and cross-referenced information
- Conducted field research

SKILLS
Adept at using several GIS systems. Excellent computer, typing, and office skills. Fluent in Japanese and Spanish.

REFERENCES
Available upon request.

Choose one of the following types of objective statement:

1. *General Objective Statement*

- An entry-level educational programming coordinator position

2. *Position-Focused Objective*

- To obtain the position of conference coordinator at State College

3. *Industry-Focused Objective*

- To begin a career as a sales representative in the cruise line industry

4. *Summary of Qualifications Statement*

A master's degree in geology and four years of progressively increasing responsibilities working for a petroleum engineering firm have prepared me for a career in resource management in an institution that values teamwork and collaboration between employees at all levels.

Support Your Objective. A résumé that contains any one of these types of objective statements should then go on to demonstrate why you are qualified to get the position. Listing academic degrees can be one way to indicate qualifications. Another demonstration would be in the way previous experiences, both volunteer and paid, are described. Without this kind of documentation in the body of the résumé, the objective looks unsupported. Think of the résumé as telling a connected story about you. All the elements should work together to form a coherent picture that ideally should relate to your statement of objective.

Education

This section of your résumé should indicate the exact name of the degree you will receive or have received, spelled out completely with no abbreviations. The degree is generally listed after the objective, followed by the institution name and location, and then the month and year of graduation. This section could also include your academic minor, grade point average (GPA), and appearance on the Dean's List or President's List.

If you have enough space, you might want to include a section listing courses related to the field in which you are seeking work. The best use of a "related courses" section would be to list some course work that is not traditionally associated with the major. Perhaps you took several computer courses outside your degree that will be helpful and related to the job prospects you are entertaining. Several education section examples are shown here:

- Master of Science Degree in Geology; University of Texas—Austin, Texas, May 2007; Concentration: Surveying; Thesis: *Geologic Mapping of the Southern Flank of the Rosillos Laccolith, Brewster County, Texas*
- Bachelor of Science in Geology; University of Missouri—Columbia, Missouri, August 2005; Minor: Spanish; GPA: 3.85 on a 4.0 scale
- Bachelor of Science Degree in Geology; Massachusetts Institute of Technology—Cambridge, MA, June 2006; Concentration: Oceanography

---

Experience

The experience section of your résumé should be the most substantial part and should take up most of the space on the page. Employers want to see what kind of work history you have. They will look at your range of experiences, longevity in jobs, and specific tasks you are able to complete. This section may also be called "work experience," "related experience," "employment history," or "employment." No matter what you call this section, some important points to remember are the following:

1. **Describe your duties** as they relate to the position you are seeking.
2. **Emphasize major responsibilities** and indicate increases in responsibility. Include all relevant employment experiences: summer, part-time, internships, cooperative education, or self-employment.
3. **Emphasize skills**, especially those that transfer from one situation to another. The fact that you coordinated a student organization, chaired meetings, supervised others, and managed a budget leads one to suspect that you could coordinate other things as well.
4. **Use descriptive job titles** that provide information about what you did. A "Student Intern" should be more specifically stated as, for example, "Magazine Operations Intern." "Volunteer" is also too general; a title such as "Peer Writing Tutor" would be more appropriate.
5. **Create word pictures** by using active verbs to start sentences. Describe *results* you have produced in the work you have done.

A limp description would say something such as the following: "My duties included helping with production, proofreading, and editing. I used a design and page layout program." An action statement would be stated as follows: "Coordinated and assisted in the creative marketing of brochures and seminar promotions, becoming proficient in Quark."

Remember, an accomplishment is simply a result, a final measurable product that people can relate to. A duty is not a result; it is an obligation—every job holder has duties. For an effective résumé, list as many results as you can. To make the most of the limited space you have and to give your description impact, carefully select appropriate and accurate descriptors.

Here are some traits that employers tell us they like to see:

- Teamwork
- Energy and motivation
- Learning and using new skills
- Versatility
- Critical thinking
- Understanding how profits are created

- Organizational acumen
- Communicating directly and clearly, in both writing and speaking
- Risk taking
- Willingness to admit mistakes
- High personal standards

Solutions to Frequently Encountered Problems

Repetitive Employment with the Same Employer
EMPLOYMENT: The Foot Locker, Portland, Oregon. Summer 2001, 2002, 2003. Initially employed in high school as salesclerk. Because of successful performance, asked to return next two summers at higher pay with added responsibility. Ranked as the #2 salesperson the first summer and #1 the next two summers. Assisted in arranging eye-catching retail displays; served as manager of other summer workers during owner's absence.

A Large Number of Jobs
EMPLOYMENT: Recent Hospitality Industry Experience: Affiliated with four upscale hotel/restaurant complexes (September 2001–February 2004), where I worked part- and full-time as a waiter, bartender, disc jockey, and bookkeeper to produce income for college.

Several Positions with the Same Employer
EMPLOYMENT: Coca-Cola Bottling Co., Burlington, Vermont, 2001–2004. In four years, I received three promotions, each with increased pay and responsibility.

Summer Sales Coordinator: Promoted to hire, train, and direct efforts of add-on staff of fifteen college-age route salespeople hired to meet summer peak demand for product.

Sales Administrator: Promoted to run home office sales desk, managing accounts and associated delivery schedules for professional sales force of ten people. Intensive phone work, daily interaction with all personnel, and strong knowledge of product line required.

Route Salesperson: Summer employment to travel and tourism industry sites that use Coke products. Met specific schedule demands, used good communication skills with wide variety of customers, and demonstrated strong selling skills. Named salesperson of the month for July and August of that year.

Questions Résumé Writers Often Ask

How Far Back Should I Go in Terms of Listing Past Jobs?

Usually, listing three or four jobs should suffice. If you did something back in high school that has a bearing on your future aspirations for employment, by all means list the job. As you progress through your college career, high school jobs will be replaced on the résumé by college employment.

Should I Differentiate Between Paid and Nonpaid Employment?

Most employers are not initially concerned about how much you were paid. They are eager to know how much responsibility you held in your past employment. There is no need to specify that your work was as a volunteer if you had significant responsibilities.

How Should I Represent My Accomplishments or Work-Related Responsibilities?

Succinctly, but fully. In other words, give the employer enough information to arouse curiosity but not so much detail that you leave nothing to the imagination. Besides, some jobs merit more lengthy explanations than others. Be sure to convey any information that can give an employer a better understanding of the depth of your involvement at work. Did you supervise others? How many? Did your efforts result in a more efficient operation? How much did you increase efficiency? Did you handle a budget? How much? Were you promoted in a short time? Did you work two jobs at once or fifteen hours per week after high school? Where appropriate, quantify.

Should the Work Section Always Follow the Education Section on the Résumé?

Always lead with your strengths. If your education closely relates to the employment you now seek, put this section after the objective. If your education does not closely relate but you have a surplus of good work experiences, consider reversing the order of your sections to lead with employment, followed by education.

How Should I Present My Activities, Honors, Awards, Professional Societies, and Affiliations?

This section of the résumé can add valuable information for an employer to consider if used correctly. The rule of thumb for information in this section is to include only those activities that are in some way relevant to the objective stated on your résumé. If you can draw a valid connection between your activities and your objective, include them; if not, leave them out.

Professional affiliations and honors should all be listed; especially important are those related to your job objective. Social clubs and activities need not be a part of your résumé unless you hold a significant office or you are looking for a position related to your membership. Be aware that most prospective employers' principal concerns are related to your employability, not your social life. If you have any, publications can be included as an addendum to your résumé.

How Should I Handle References?

The use of references is considered a part of the interview process, and they should never be listed on a résumé. You would always provide references to a potential employer if requested to, so it is not even necessary to include this section on the résumé if space does not permit. If space is available, it is acceptable to include the following statement:

- References furnished upon request.

The Functional Résumé

The functional résumé departs from a chronological résumé in that it organizes information by specific accomplishments in various settings: previous jobs, volunteer work, associations, and so forth. This type of résumé permits you to stress the substance of your experiences rather than the position titles you have held. You should consider using a functional résumé if you have held a series of similar jobs that relied on the same skills or abilities. There are many good books in which you can find examples of functional résumés, including *How to Write a Winning Resume* or *Resumes Made Easy*.

The Targeted Résumé

The targeted résumé focuses on specific work-related capabilities you can bring to a given position within an organization. Past achievements are listed to highlight your capabilities and the work history section is abbreviated.

Digital Résumés

Today's employers have to manage an enormous number of résumés. One of the most frequent complaints the writers of this series hear from students is the failure of employers to even acknowledge the receipt of a résumé and cover letter. Frequently, the reason for this poor response or nonresponse is the volume of applications received for every job. In an attempt to better manage the considerable labor investment involved in processing large numbers of résumés, many employers are requiring digital submission of résumés. There are two types of digital résumés: those that can be e-mailed or posted to a website, called *electronic résumés*, and those that can be "read" by a computer, commonly called *scannable résumés*. Though the format may be a bit different from the traditional "paper" résumé, the goal of both types of digital résumés is the same—to get you an interview! These résumés must be designed to be "technologically friendly." What that basically means to you is that they should be free of graphics and fancy formatting. (See Exhibit 2.2.)

Electronic Résumés

Sometimes referred to as plain-text résumés, electronic résumés are designed to be e-mailed to an employer or posted to one of many commercial Internet databases such as CareerMosaic.com, America's Job Bank (ajb.dni.us), or Monster.com.

Some technical considerations:

- Electronic résumés must be written in American Standard Code for Information Interchange (ASCII), which is simply a plain-text format. These characters are universally recognized so that every computer can accurately read and understand them. To create an ASCII file of your current résumé, open your document, then save it as a text or ASCII file. This will eliminate all formatting. Edit as needed using your computer's text editor application.

Exhibit 2.2
DIGITAL RÉSUMÉ

RENEE BROWN
3228 N. Seminary Ave.
Chicago, IL 60647
(773) 555-0643
rbrown@xxx.com

Put your name at the
top on its own line.

Put your phone number
on its own line.

KEYWORD SUMMARY
Environmental research
GIS systems
Geology
Technology

Keywords make your
résumé easier to find in
a database.

EDUCATION
University of Chicago. Chicago, IL.
    Dec 2002 to Dec 2006
B.S. Environmental Earth Resources
Major GPA: 4.0
Sigma Theta Tau Geological Honors Society member

Use a standard-width
typeface.

RELEVANT COURSES
* Advanced Geographic Information System
* Remote Sensing Technology
* Seismic Geology
* Preparation of Environmental Impact Statements

No line should exceed
sixty-five characters.

EXPERIENCE
Department Head Assistant. Oct 2003 to Nov 2006.
University of Chicago. Department of Geology.
Kept schedules, filed papers, manuscript preparation.
Attended lectures and research symposiums.

Capitalize letters to
emphasize heading

End each line by
hitting the ENTER
(or RETURN) key.

- Use a standard-width typeface. Courier is a good choice because it is the font associated with ASCII in most systems.
- Use a font size of 11 to 14 points. A 12-point font is considered standard.
- Your margin should be left-justified.
- Do not exceed sixty-five characters per line because the word-wrap function doesn't operate in ASCII.
- Do not use boldface, italics, underlining, bullets, or various font sizes. Instead, use asterisks, plus signs, or all capital letters when you want to emphasize something.
- Avoid graphics and shading.
- Use as many "keywords" as you possibly can. These are words or phrases usually relating to skills or experience that either are specifically used in the job announcement or are popular buzzwords in the industry.
- Minimize abbreviations.
- Your name should be the first line of text.
- Conduct a "test run" by e-mailing your résumé to yourself and a friend before you send it to the employer. See how it transmits, and make any changes you need to. Continue to test it until it's exactly how you want it to look.
- Unless an employer specifically requests that you send the résumé in the form of an attachment, don't. Employers can encounter problems opening a document as an attachment, and there are always viruses to consider.
- Don't forget your cover letter. Send it along with your résumé as a single message.

Scannable Résumés

Some companies are relying on technology to narrow the candidate pool for available job openings. Electronic Applicant Tracking uses imaging to scan, sort, and store résumé elements in a database. Then, through OCR (Optical Character Recognition) software, the computer scans the résumés for keywords and phrases. To have the best chance at getting an interview, you want to increase the number of "hits"—matches of your skills, abilities, experience, and education to those the computer is scanning for—your résumé will get. You can see how critical using the right keywords is for this type of résumé.

Technical considerations include:

- Again, do not use boldface (newer systems may be able to read this, but many older ones won't), italics, underlining, bullets, shading, graphics, or multiple font sizes. Instead, for emphasis, use asterisks, plus signs, or all capital letters. Minimize abbreviations.
- Use a popular typeface such as Courier, Helvetica, Ariel, or Palatino. Avoid decorative fonts.
- Font size should be between 11 and 14 points.
- Do not compress the spacing between letters.
- Use horizontal and vertical lines sparingly; the computer may misread them as the letters *L* or *I*.
- Left-justify the text.
- Do not use parentheses or brackets around telephone numbers, and be sure your phone number is on its own line of text.
- Your name should be the first line of text and on its own line. If your résumé is longer than one page, be sure to put your name on the top of all pages.
- Use a traditional résumé structure. The chronological format may work best.
- Use nouns that are skill-focused, such as *management, writer*, and *programming*. This is different from traditional paper résumés, which use action-oriented verbs.
- Laser printers produce the finest copies. Avoid dot-matrix printers.
- Use standard, light-colored paper with text on one side only. Since the higher the contrast, the better, your best choice is black ink on white paper.
- Always send original copies. If you must fax, set the fax on fine mode, not standard.
- Do not staple or fold your résumé. This can confuse the computer.
- Before you send your scannable résumé, be certain the employer uses this technology. If you can't determine this, you may want to send two versions (scannable and traditional) to be sure your résumé gets considered.

Résumé Production and Other Tips

An ink-jet printer is the preferred option for printing your résumé. Begin by printing just a few copies. You may find a small error or you may simply want to make some changes, and it is less frustrating and less expensive if you print in small batches.

Résumé paper color should be carefully chosen. You should consider the types of employers who will receive your résumé and the types of positions for which you are applying. Use white or ivory paper for traditional or conservative employers or for higher-level positions.

Black ink on sharp, white paper can be harsh on the reader's eyes. Think about an ivory or cream paper that will provide less contrast and be easier to read. Pink, green, and blue tints should generally be avoided.

Many résumé writers buy packages of matching envelopes and cover sheet stationery that, although not absolutely necessary, help convey a professional impression.

If you'll be producing many cover letters at home, be sure you have high-quality printing equipment. Learn standard envelope formats for business, and retain a copy of every cover letter you send out. You can use the copies to take notes of any telephone conversations that may occur.

If attending a job fair, either carry a briefcase or place your résumé in a nicely covered legal-size pad holder.

The Cover Letter

The cover letter provides you with the opportunity to tailor your résumé by telling the prospective employer how you can be a benefit to the organization. It allows you to highlight aspects of your background that are not already discussed in your résumé and that might be especially relevant to the organization you are contacting or to the position you are seeking. Every résumé should have a cover letter enclosed when you send it out. Unlike the résumé, which may be mass-produced, a cover letter is most effective when it is individually prepared and focused on the particular requirements of the organization in question.

A good cover letter should supplement the résumé and motivate the reader to review the résumé. The format shown in Exhibit 2.3 (see page 34) is only a suggestion to help you decide what information to include in a cover letter.

Begin the cover letter with your street address six lines down from the top. Leave three to five lines between the date and the name of the person to whom you are addressing the cover letter. Make sure you leave one blank line between the salutation and the body of the letter and between paragraphs. After typing "Sincerely," leave four blank lines and type your name.

This should leave plenty of room for your signature. A sample cover letter is shown in Exhibit 2.4 on page 35.

The following guidelines will help you write good cover letters:

1. Be sure to type your letter neatly; ensure there are no misspellings.
2. Avoid unusual typefaces, such as script.
3. Address the letter to an individual, using the person's name and title. To obtain this information, call the company. If answering a blind newspaper advertisement, address the letter "To Whom It May Concern" or omit the salutation.
4. Be sure your cover letter directly indicates the position you are applying for and tells why you are qualified to fill it.
5. Send the original letter, not a photocopy, with your résumé. Keep a copy for your records.
6. Make your cover letter no more than one page.
7. Include a phone number where you can be reached.
8. Avoid trite language and have someone read the letter over to react to its tone, content, and mechanics.
9. For your own information, record the date you send out each letter and résumé.

Exhibit 2.3
COVER LETTER FORMAT

Your Street Address
Your Town, State, Zip
Phone Number
Fax Number
E-mail

Date

Name
Title
Organization
Address

Dear _____:

First Paragraph. In this paragraph state the reason for the letter, name the specific position or type of work you are applying for, and indicate from which resource (career services office, website, newspaper, contact, employment service) you learned of this opening. The first paragraph can also be used to inquire about future openings.

Second Paragraph. Indicate why you are interested in this position, the company, or its products or services and what you can do for the employer. If you are a recent graduate, explain how your academic background makes you a qualified candidate. Try not to repeat the same information found in the résumé.

Third Paragraph. Refer the reader to the enclosed résumé for more detailed information.

Fourth Paragraph. In this paragraph say what you will do to follow up on your letter. For example, state that you will call by a certain date to set up an interview or to find out if the company will be recruiting in your area. Finish by indicating your willingness to answer any questions the recipient may have. Be sure you have provided your phone number.

Sincerely,

Type your name

Enclosure

Exhibit 2.4
SAMPLE COVER LETTER

150 Oak Street
Brighton, MA 02135
(617) 555-8443

July 1, 2006

Ms. Eliza Taylor
Vice President for Human Resources
Colorado Earth Science
P.O. Box 3211
Denver 87504

Dear Ms. Taylor:

I am a recent graduate of Northeastern University with a bachelor of science degree in geology and a master of science degree in museum studies. I am interested in the assistant collections manager position available at Sterling Museum of Natural History, and I believe that I would make an excellent addition to your team.

Through my three-year placement at the Boston Museum of Natural History with Northeastern's cooperative education program, I learned the ins and outs of working for a major museum, including the importance of teamwork. Under the direction of the curator of collections, I gained valuable experience handling and exhibiting minerals and fossils and understanding what piques the public's interest. You should also know that I am a creative individual and a fast learner. I enjoy working collaboratively with others and with the public. I possess excellent communication skills and collection management experience.

In addition to the various geology and museum studies courses in my academic program, I completed several computer science and systems courses and am adept at spreadsheet and database design and management. I believe that, coupled with my enthusiasm for working in a natural history museum

continued

environment, these traits will help me to represent your fine establishment in a professional and enthusiastic manner.

I would appreciate the opportunity to meet with you to discuss how my education and experience could benefit your department and the museum. I will contact your office next week to discuss the possibility of an interview. In the meantime, enclosed is my Résumé for your review. If you have any questions or require additional information, please contact me at my home at (617) 555-8443.

All best wishes,

Susan Smith

Enclosure

3

Researching Careers and Networking

What do they call the job you want? One reason for confusion is perhaps a mistaken assumption that a college education provides job training. In most cases it does not. Of course, applied fields such as engineering, management, or education provide specific skills for the workplace as well as an education. Regardless, your overall college education exposes you to numerous fields of study and teaches you quantitative reasoning, critical thinking, writing, and speaking, all of which can be successfully applied to a number of different job fields. But it still remains up to you to choose a job field and to learn how to articulate the benefits of your education in a way the employer will appreciate.

One common question a career counselor encounters is "What can I do with my degree?" Geology majors have narrowed down their interests a little more successfully than others, but still, all the choices are not clearly defined. Geology is a wide field, populated with scores of job titles you might never have heard of before. You know that geology majors can go into museum work, teaching and research, environmental work, the oil and gas fields, or the mining industry, to name just the major paths. However, you may still be confused as to exactly what kinds of jobs you can do with your degree, what your duties will be, and what kinds of organizations will hire you. Where does a geology major fit into an environmental consulting firm? What does a geology major actually do for a mining operation, an oil company, or a natural history museum?

Collect Job Titles

The world of employment is a complex place, so you need to become a bit of an explorer and adventurer and be willing to try a variety of techniques to develop a list of possible occupations that might use your talents and education. You might find computerized interest inventories, reference books and other sources, and classified ads helpful in this respect. Once you have a list of possibilities that you are interested in and qualified for, you can move on to find out what kinds of organizations have these job titles.

Computerized Interest Inventories. One way to begin collecting job titles is to identify a number of jobs that call for your degree and the particular skills and interests you identified as part of the self-assessment process. There are excellent interactive career-guidance programs on the market to help you produce such selected lists of possible job titles. Most of these are available at colleges and at some larger town and city libraries. Two of the industry leaders are *CHOICES* and *DISCOVER*. Both allow you to enter interests, values, educational background, and other information to produce lists of possible occupations and industries. Each of the resources listed here will produce different job title lists. Some job titles will appear again and again, while others will be unique to a particular source. Investigate all of them!

Reference Sources. Books on the market that may be available through your local library or career counseling office also suggest various occupations related to specific majors. The following are only a few of the many good books on the market: *The College Board Guide to 150 Popular College Majors* and *College Majors and Careers: A Resource Guide for Effective Life Planning* both by Paul Phifer, and *Kaplan's What to Study: 101 Fields in a Flash*. All of these books list possible job titles within the academic major.

Not every employer seeking to hire someone with a geology degree may be equally desirable to you. Some employment environments may be more attractive than others. An environmental geologist, for example, who wants to reclaim damaged land sites could do so working for a private contractor, a government agency, or within a non-profit firm. Each of these environments presents a different "culture," with associated norms in the pace of work, the subject matter of interest, and the outlook and backgrounds of its employees. Although the job titles may be the same, not all locations present the same "fit" for you.

If you majored in geology, specializing in hydrogeology, and enjoyed the fieldwork you participated in as part of your course work, you might think that you'll be happiest doing field research. But geology majors with these same skills and interests might go on to teach others their skills or to work for the government or private environmental or engineering firms. Keep in mind that the work you enjoy can be found in a number of different settings.

Each job title deserves your consideration. Like removing the layers of an onion, the search for job titles can go on and on! As you spend time doing this activity, you are actually learning more about the value of your degree. What's important in your search at this point is not to become critical or selective but rather to develop as long a list of possibilities as you can. Every source used will help you add new and potentially exciting jobs to your growing list.

Classified Ads. It has been well publicized that the classified ad section of the newspaper represents only a small fraction of the current job market. Nevertheless, the weekly classified ads can be a great help to you in your search. Although they may not be the best place to look for a job, they can teach you a lot about the job market. Classified ads provide a good education in job descriptions, duties, responsibilities, and qualifications. In addition, they provide insight into which industries are actively recruiting and some indication of the area's employment market. This is particularly helpful when seeking a position in a specific geographic area and/or a specific field. For your purposes, classified ads are a good source for job titles to add to your list.

Read the Sunday classified ads in a major market newspaper for several weeks in a row. Cut and paste all the ads that interest you and seem to call for something close to your education, skills, experience, and interests. Remember that classified ads are written for what an organization *hopes* to find; you don't have to meet absolutely every criterion. However, if certain requirements are stated as absolute minimums and you cannot meet them, it's best not to waste your time and that of the employer.

The weekly classified want ads exercise is important because these jobs are out in the marketplace. They truly exist, and people with your qualifications are being sought to apply. What's more, many of these advertisements describe the duties and responsibilities of the job advertised and give you a beginning sense of the challenges and opportunities such a position presents. Some will indicate salary, and that will be helpful as well. This information will better define the jobs for you and provide some good material for possible interviews in that field.

Explore Job Descriptions

Once you've arrived at a solid list of possible job titles that interest you and for which you believe you are somewhat qualified, it's a good idea to do some research on each of these jobs. The preeminent source for such job information is the *Dictionary of Occupational Titles*, or *DOT* (wave.net/upg/immigration/dot_index.html). This directory lists every conceivable job and provides excellent up-to-date information on duties and responsibilities, interactions with associates, and day-to-day assignments and tasks. These descriptions provide a thorough job analysis, but they do not consider the possible employers or the environments in which a job may be performed. So, although a position as public relations officer may be well defined in terms of duties and responsibilities, it does not explain the differences in doing public relations work in a college or a hospital or a factory or a bank. You will need to look somewhere else for work settings.

Learn More About Possible Work Settings

After reading some job descriptions, you may choose to edit and revise your list of job titles once again, discarding those you feel are not suitable and keeping those that continue to hold your interest. Or you may wish to keep your list intact and see where these jobs may be located. For example, if you are interested in public relations and you appear to have those skills and the requisite education, you'll want to know which organizations do public relations. How can you find that out? How much income does someone in public relations make a year and what is the employment potential for the field of public relations?

To answer these and many other questions about your list of job titles, we recommend you try any of the following resources: *Careers Encyclopedia*, the professional societies and resources found throughout this book, *College to Career: The Guide to Job Opportunities*, and the *Occupational Outlook Handbook* (http://stats.bls.gov/ocohome.htm). Each of these resources, in a different way, will help to put the job titles you have selected into an employer context. Perhaps the most extensive discussion is found in the *Occupational Outlook Handbook*, which gives a thorough presentation of the nature of the work, the working conditions, employment statistics, training, other qualifications, and advancement possibilities as well as job outlook and earnings. Related occupations are also detailed, and a select bibliography is provided to help you find additional information.

Continuing with our public relations example, your search through these reference materials would teach you that the public relations jobs you find attractive are available in larger hospitals, financial institutions, most corporations (both consumer goods and industrial goods), media organizations, and colleges and universities.

Networking

Networking is the process of deliberately establishing relationships to get career-related information or to alert potential employers that you are available for work. Networking is critically important to today's job seeker for two reasons: It will help you get the information you need, and it can help you find out about *all* of the available jobs.

Get the Information You Need

Networkers will review your résumé and give you feedback on its effectiveness. They will talk about the job you are looking for and give you a candid appraisal of how they see your strengths and weaknesses. If they have a good sense of the industry or the employment sector for that job, you'll get their feelings on future trends in the industry as well. Some networkers will be very forthcoming about salaries, job-hunting techniques, and suggestions for your job search strategy. Many have been known to place calls right from the interview desk to friends and associates who might be interested in you. Each networker will make his or her own contribution, and each will be valuable.

Because organizations must evolve to adapt to current global market needs, the information provided by decision makers within various organizations will be critical to your success as a new job market entrant. For example, you might learn about the concept of virtual organizations from a networker. Virtual organizations coordinate economic activity to deliver value to customers by using resources outside the traditional boundaries of the organization. This concept is being discussed and implemented by chief executive officers of many organizations, including Ford Motor, Dell, and IBM. Networking can help you find out about this and other trends currently affecting the industries under your consideration.

Find Out About All of the Available Jobs

Not every job that is available at this very moment is advertised for potential applicants to see. This is called the *hidden job market*. Only 15 to 20 percent of all jobs are formally advertised, which means that 80 to 85 percent of available jobs do not appear in published channels. Networking will help you become more knowledgeable about all the employment opportunities available during your job search period.

Although someone you might talk to today doesn't know of any openings within his or her organization, tomorrow or next week or next month an opening may occur. If you've taken the time to show an interest in and knowledge of their organization, if you've shown the company representative how you can help achieve organizational goals and that you can fit into the organization, you'll be one of the first candidates considered for the position.

Networking: A Proactive Approach

Networking is a proactive rather than a reactive approach. You, as a job seeker, are expected to initiate a certain level of activity on your own behalf; you cannot afford to simply respond to jobs listed in the newspaper. Being proactive means building a network of contacts that includes informed and interested decision makers who will provide you with up-to-date knowledge of the current job market and increase your chances of finding out about employment opportunities appropriate for your interests, experience, and level of education. An old axiom of networking says, "You are only two phone calls away from the information you need." In other words, by talking to enough people, you will quickly come across someone who can offer you help.

Preparing to Network

In deliberately establishing relationships, maximize your efforts by organizing your approach. Five specific areas in which you can organize your efforts include reviewing your self-assessment, reviewing your research on job sites and organizations, deciding whom you want to talk to, keeping track of all your efforts, and creating your self-promotion tools.

Review Your Self-Assessment

Your self-assessment is as important a tool in preparing to network as it has been in other aspects of your job search. You have carefully evaluated your personal traits, personal values, economic needs, longer-term goals, skill base, preferred skills, and underdeveloped skills. During the networking process you will be called upon to communicate what you know about yourself and relate it to the information or job you seek. Be sure to review the exercises that you completed in the self-assessment section of this book in preparation for networking. We've explained that you need to assess which skills you have acquired from your major that are of general value to an employer; be ready to express those in ways he or she can appreciate as useful in the organizations.

Review Research on Job Sites and Organizations

In addition, individuals assisting you will expect that you'll have at least some background information on the occupation or industry of interest to you. Refer to the appropriate sections of this book and other relevant publications to acquire the background information necessary for effective networking. They'll explain how to identify not only the job titles that might be of interest to you but also which kinds of organizations employ people to do that job. You will develop some sense of working conditions and expectations about duties and responsibilities—all of which will be of help in your networking interviews.

Decide Whom You Want to Talk To

Networking cannot begin until you decide whom you want to talk to and, in general, what type of information you hope to gain from your contacts. Once you know this, it's time to begin developing a list of contacts. Five useful sources for locating contacts are described here.

College Alumni Network. Most colleges and universities have created a formal network of alumni and friends of the institution who are particularly interested in helping currently enrolled students and graduates of their alma mater gain employment-related information.

It is usually a simple process to make use of an alumni network. Visit your college's website and locate the alumni office and/or your career center. Either or both sites will have information about your school's alumni network. You'll be provided with information on shadowing experiences, geographic information, or those alumni offering job referrals. If you don't find what you're looking for, don't hesitate to phone or e-mail your career center and ask what they can do to help you connect with an alum.

Alumni networkers may provide some combination of the following services: day-long shadowing experiences, telephone interviews, in-person interviews, information on relocating to given geographic areas, internship information, suggestions on graduate school study, and job vacancy notices.

Present and Former Supervisors. If you believe you are on good terms with present or former job supervisors, they may be an excellent resource for providing information or directing you to appropriate resources that would have information related to your current interests and needs. Additionally, these supervisors probably belong to professional organizations that they might be willing to utilize to get information for you.

Employers in Your Area. Although you may be interested in working in a geographic location different from the one where you currently reside, don't overlook the value of the knowledge and contacts those around you are able to provide. Use the local telephone directory and newspaper to identify the types of organizations you are thinking of working for or professionals who have the kinds of jobs you are interested in. Recently, a call made to a local hospital's financial administrator for information on working in health-care financial administration yielded more pertinent information on training seminars, regional professional organizations, and potential employment sites than a national organization was willing to provide.

Employers in Geographic Areas Where You Hope to Work. If you are thinking about relocating, identifying prospective employers or informational contacts in the new location will be critical to your success. Here are some tips for online searching. First, use a "metasearch" engine to get the most out of your search. Metasearch engines combine several engines into one powerful tool. We frequently use dogpile.com and metasearch.com for this purpose. Try using the city and state as your keywords in a search. *New Haven, Connecticut* will bring you to the city's website with links to the chamber of commerce, member businesses, and other valuable resources. By using looksmart.com you can locate newspapers in any area, and they, too, can provide valuable insight before you relocate. Of course, both dogpile and metasearch can lead you to yellow and white page directories in areas you are considering.

Professional Associations and Organizations. Professional associations and organizations can provide valuable information in several areas: career paths that you might not have considered, qualifications relating to those career choices, publications that list current job openings, and workshops or seminars that will enhance your professional knowledge and skills. They can also be excellent sources for background information on given industries: their health, current problems, and future challenges.

There are several excellent resources available to help you locate professional associations and organizations that would have information to meet your needs. Two especially useful publications are the *Encyclopedia of Associations* and *National Trade and Professional Associations of the United States.*

Keep Track of All Your Efforts

It can be difficult, almost impossible, to remember all the details related to each contact you make during the networking process, so you will want to develop a record-keeping system that works for you. Formalize this process by using your computer to keep a record of the people and organizations you want to contact. You can simply record the contact's name, address, and telephone number, and what information you hope to gain.

You could record this as a simple Word document and you could still use the "Find" function if you were trying to locate some data and could only recall the firm's name or the contact's name. If you're comfortable with database management and you have some database software on your computer, then you can put information at your fingertips even if you have only the zip code! The point here is not technological sophistication but good record keeping.

Once you have created this initial list, it will be helpful to keep more detailed information as you begin to actually make the contacts. Those details should include complete contact information, the date and content of each contact, names and information for additional networkers, and required follow-up. Don't forget to send a letter thanking your contact for his or her time! Your contact will appreciate your recall of details of your meetings and conversations, and the information will help you to focus your networking efforts.

Create Your Self-Promotion Tools

There are two types of promotional tools that are used in the networking process. The first is a résumé and cover letter, and the second is a one-minute "infomercial," which may be given over the telephone or in person.

Techniques for writing an effective résumé and cover letter are discussed in Chapter 2. Once you have reviewed that material and prepared these important documents, you will have created one of your self-promotion tools.

The one-minute infomercial will demand that you begin tying your interests, abilities, and skills to the people or organizations you want to network with. Think about your goal for making the contact to help you understand what you should say about yourself. You should be able to express yourself easily and convincingly. If, for example, you are contacting an alumnus of your institution to obtain the names of possible employment sites in a distant city, be prepared to discuss why you are interested in moving to that location, the types of jobs you are interested in, and the skills and abilities you possess that will make you a qualified candidate.

To create a meaningful one-minute infomercial, write it out, practice it as if it will be a spoken presentation, rewrite it, and practice it again if necessary until expressing yourself comes easily and is convincing.

Here's a simplified example of an infomercial for use over the telephone:

Hello, Dr. Frank? My name is Jordan Stoll and I am a recent graduate of the University of Michigan. I was a medical geology major and I possess many of the skills that are valued in the healthcare industry, including analytical and research skills, as well as community outreach experience.

I know you're extremely busy, so I'll get to the point. I'm calling today because I would like to gather more information about the work medical geologists do in the healthcare field to make sure that I'm making the best career choice for me. I'm hoping you'll have some time to sit down with me for about half an hour and discuss your perspective on medical geology careers. Would you be willing to do that for me?

I would greatly appreciate any time you're able to offer me. I am available most mornings, if that's good for you.

It very well may happen that your employer contact wishes you to communicate by e-mail. The infomercial quoted above could easily be rewritten for an e-mail message. You should "cut and paste" your résumé right into the e-mail text itself.

Other effective self-promotion tools include portfolios for those in the arts, writing professions, or teaching. Portfolios show examples of work, photographs of projects or classroom activities, or certificates and credentials that are job related. There may not be an opportunity to use the portfolio during an interview, and it is not something that should be left with the organization. It is designed to be explained and displayed by the creator. However, during some networking meetings, there may be an opportunity to illustrate a point or strengthen a qualification by exhibiting the portfolio.

Beginning the Networking Process

Set the Tone for Your Communications
It can be useful to establish "tone words" for any communications you embark upon. Before making your first telephone call or writing your first letter, decide what you want the person to think of you. If you are networking to try to obtain a job, your tone words might include descriptors such as *genuine*, *informed*, and *self-knowledgeable*. When you're trying to acquire information, your tone words may have a slightly different focus, such as *courteous*, *organized*, *focused*, and *well-spoken*. Use the tone words you establish for your contacts to guide you through the networking process.

Honestly Express Your Intentions
When contacting individuals, it is important to be honest about your reasons for making the contact. Establish your purpose in your own mind and be able and ready to articulate it concisely. Determine an initial agenda, whether it be informational questioning or self-promotion, present it to your contact, and be ready to respond immediately. If you don't adequately prepare before initiating your overture, you may find yourself at a disadvantage if you're asked to immediately begin your informational interview or self-promotion during the first phone conversation or visit.

Start Networking Within Your Circle of Confidence
Once you have organized your approach—by utilizing specific researching methods, creating a system for keeping track of the people you will contact, and developing effective self-promotion tools—you are ready to begin networking. The best way to begin networking is by talking with a group of people you trust and feel comfortable with. This group is usually made up of your family, friends, and career counselors. No matter who is in this inner circle, they will have a special interest in seeing you succeed in your job search. In addition, because they will be easy to talk to, you should try taking some risks in terms of practicing your information-seeking approach. Gain confidence in talking about the strengths you bring to an organization and the underdeveloped skills you feel hinder your candidacy. Be sure to review the section on self-assessment for tips on approaching each of these areas. Ask for critical but constructive feedback from the people in your circle of confidence on the letters you write and the one-minute infomercial you have

developed. Evaluate whether you want to make the changes they suggest, then practice the changes on others within this circle.

Stretch the Boundaries of Your Networking Circle of Confidence

Once you have refined the promotional tools you will use to accomplish your networking goals, you will want to make additional contacts. Because you will not know most of these people, it will be a less comfortable activity to undertake. The practice that you gained with your inner circle of trusted friends should have prepared you to now move outside of that comfort zone.

It is said that any information a person needs is only two phone calls away, but the information cannot be gained until you (1) make a reasonable guess about who might have the information you need and (2) pick up the telephone to make the call. Using your network list that includes alumni, instructors, supervisors, employers, and associations, you can begin preparing your list of questions that will allow you to get the information you need.

Prepare the Questions You Want to Ask

Networkers can provide you with the insider's perspective on any given field and you can ask them questions that you might not want to ask in an interview. For example, you can ask them to describe the more repetitive or mundane parts of the job or ask them for a realistic idea of salary expectations. Be sure to prepare your questions ahead of time so that you are organized and efficient.

Be Prepared to Answer Some Questions

To communicate effectively, you must anticipate questions that will be asked of you by the networkers you contact. Revisit the self-assessment process you undertook and the research you've done so that you can effortlessly respond to questions about your short- and long-term goals and the kinds of jobs you are most interested in pursuing.

General Networking Tips

Make Every Contact Count. Setting the tone for each interaction is critical. Approaches that will help you communicate in an effective way include politeness, being appreciative of time provided to you, and being prepared and thorough. Remember, *everyone* within an organization has a circle of influence, so be prepared to interact effectively with each person you encounter in the networking process, including secretarial and support staff. Many information or job seekers have thwarted their own efforts by being rude to some individuals they encountered as they networked because they made the incorrect assumption that certain persons were unimportant.

Sometimes your contacts may be surprised at their ability to help you. After meeting and talking with you, they might think they have not offered much in the way of help. A day or two later, however, they may make a contact that would be useful to you and refer you to that person.

With Each Contact, Widen Your Circle of Networkers. Always leave an informational interview with the names of at least two more people who can help you get the information or job that you are seeking. Don't be shy about asking for additional contacts; networking is all about increasing the number of people you can interact with to achieve your goals.

Make Your Own Decisions. As you talk with different people and get answers to the questions you pose, you may hear conflicting information or get conflicting suggestions. Your job is to listen to these "experts" and decide what information and which suggestions will help you achieve *your* goals. Only implement those suggestions that you believe will work for you.

Shutting Down Your Network

As you achieve the goals that motivated your networking activity—getting the information you need or the job you want—the time will come to inactivate all or parts of your network. As you do, be sure to tell your primary supporters about your change in status. Call or write to each one of them and give them as many details about your new status as you feel is necessary to maintain a positive relationship.

Because a network takes on a life of its own, activity undertaken on your behalf will continue even after you cease your efforts. As you get calls or are contacted in some fashion, be sure to inform these networkers about your change in status, and thank them for assistance they have provided.

Information on the latest employment trends indicates that workers will change jobs or careers several times in their lifetime. Networking, then, will be a critical aspect in the span of your professional life. If you carefully and thoughtfully conduct your networking activities during your job search, you will have a solid foundation of experience when you need to network the next time around.

Where Are These Jobs, Anyway?

Having a list of job titles that you've designed around your own career interests and skills is an excellent beginning. It means you've really thought about who you are and what you are presenting to the employment market. It has caused you to think seriously about the most appealing environments to work in, and you have identified some employer types that represent these environments.

The research and the thinking that you've done thus far will be used again and again. They will be helpful in writing your résumé and cover letters, in talking about yourself on the telephone to prospective employers, and in answering interview questions.

Now is a good time to begin to narrow the field of job titles and employment sites down to some specific employers to initiate the employment contact.

Find Out Which Employers Hire People Like You

This section will provide tips, techniques, and specific resources for developing an actual list of specific employers that can be used to make contacts. It is only an outline that you must be prepared to tailor to your own particular needs and according to what you bring to the job search. Once again, it is important to communicate with others along the way exactly what you're looking for and what your goals are for the research you're doing. Librarians, employers, career counselors, friends, friends of friends, business contacts, and bookstore staff will all have helpful information on geographically specific and new resources to aid you in locating employers who'll hire you.

Identify Information Resources

Your interview wardrobe and your new résumé might have put a dent in your wallet, but the resources you'll need to pursue your job search are available for free. The categories of information detailed here are not hard to find and are yours for the browsing.

Numerous resources described in this section will help you identify actual employers. Use all of them or any others that you identify as available in your geographic area. As you become experienced in this process, you'll quickly figure out which information sources are helpful and which are not. If you live in a rural area, a well-planned day trip to a major city that includes a college career office, a large college or city library, state and federal employment centers, a chamber of commerce office, and a well-stocked bookstore can produce valuable results.

There are many excellent resources available to help you identify actual job sites. They are categorized into employer directories (usually indexed by product lines and geographic location), geographically based directories (designed to highlight particular cities, regions, or states), career-specific directories (e.g., *Sports MarketPlace*, which lists tens of thousands of firms involved with sports), periodicals and newspapers, targeted job posting publications, and videos. This is by no means meant to be a complete treatment of resources but rather a starting point for identifying useful resources.

Working from the more general references to highly specific resources, we provide a basic list to help you begin your search. Many of these you'll find easily available. In some cases reference librarians and others will suggest even better materials for your particular situation. Start to create your own customized bibliography of job search references.

Geographically Based Directories. The Job Bank series published by Bob Adams, Inc. (aip.com) contains detailed entries on each area's major employers, including business activity, address, phone number, and hiring contact name. Many listings specify educational backgrounds being sought in potential employees. Each volume contains a solid discussion of each city's or state's major employment sectors. Organizations are also indexed by industry. Job Bank volumes are available for the following places: Atlanta, Boston, Chicago, Dallas–Ft. Worth, Denver, Detroit, Florida, Houston, Los Angeles, Minneapolis, New York, Ohio, Philadelphia, San Francisco, Seattle, St. Louis, Washington, D.C., and other cities throughout the Northwest.

National Job Bank (careercity.com) lists employers in every state, along with contact names and commonly hired job categories. Included are many small companies often overlooked by other directories. Companies are also indexed by industry. This publication provides information on educational backgrounds sought and lists company benefits.

Periodicals and Newspapers. Several sources are available to help you locate which journals or magazines carry job advertisements in your field. Other resources help you identify opportunities in other parts of the country.

- *Where the Jobs Are: A Comprehensive Directory of 1200 Journals Listing Career Opportunities*
- *Corptech Fast 5000 Company Locator*

- *National Ad Search* (nationaladsearch.com)
- *The Federal Jobs Digest* (jobsfed.com) and *Federal Career Opportunities*
- *World Chamber of Commerce Directory* (chamberofcommerce.org)

This list is certainly not exhaustive; use it to begin your job search work.

Targeted Job Posting Publications. Although the resources that follow are national in scope, they are either targeted to one medium of contact (telephone), focused on specific types of jobs, or less comprehensive than the sources previously listed.

- Careers.org (careers.org/index.html)
- *The Job Hunter* (jobhunter.com)
- *Current Jobs for Graduates* (graduatejobs.com)
- *Environmental Opportunities* (ecojobs.com)
- *Y National Vacancy List* (ymca.net/employment/ymca_recruiting/jobright.htm)
- *ArtSEARCH*
- *Community Jobs*
- *National Association of Colleges and Employers: Job Choices series*
- *National Association of Colleges and Employers* (jobweb.com)

Videos. You may be one of the many job seekers who likes to get information via a medium other than paper. Many career libraries, public libraries, and career centers in libraries carry an assortment of videos that will help you learn new techniques and get information helpful in the job search.

Locate Information Resources

Throughout these introductory chapters, we have continually referred you to various websites for information on everything from job listings to career information. Using the Web gives you a mobility at your computer that you don't enjoy if you rely solely on books or newspapers or printed journals. Moreover, material on the Web, if the site is maintained, can be the most up-to-date information available.

You'll eventually identify the information resources that work best for you, but make certain you've covered the full range of resources before you begin to rely on a smaller list. Here's a short list of informational sites that many job seekers find helpful:

- Public and college libraries
- College career centers

- Bookstores
- The Internet
- Local and state government personnel offices
- Career/job fairs

Each one of these sites offers a collection of resources that will help you get the information you need.

As you meet and talk with service professionals at all these sites, be sure to let them know what you're doing. Inform them of your job search, what you've already accomplished, and what you're looking for. The more people who know you're job seeking, the greater the possibility that someone will have information or know someone who can help you along your way.

4

Interviewing and Job Offer Considerations

Certainly, there can be no one part of the job search process more fraught with anxiety and worry than the interview. Yet seasoned job seekers welcome the interview and will often say, "Just get me an interview and I'm on my way!" They understand that the interview is crucial to the hiring process and equally crucial for them, as job candidates, to have the opportunity of a personal dialogue to add to what the employer may already have learned from the résumé, cover letter, and telephone conversations.

Believe it or not, the interview is to be welcomed, and even enjoyed! It is a perfect opportunity for you, the candidate, to sit down with an employer and express yourself and display who you are and what you want. Of course, it takes thought and planning and a little strategy; after all, it *is* a job interview! But it can be a positive, if not pleasant, experience and one you can look back on and feel confident about your performance and effort.

For many new job seekers, a job, any job, seems a wonderful thing. But seasoned interview veterans know that the job interview is an important step for both sides—the employer and the candidate—to see what each has to offer and whether there is going to be a "fit" of personalities, work styles, and attitudes. And it is this concept of balance in the interview, that both sides have important parts to play, that holds the key to success in mastering this aspect of the job search strategy.

Try to think of the interview as a conversation between two interested and equal partners. You both have important, even vital, information to deliver and to learn. Of course, there's no denying the employer has some leverage, especially in the initial interview for recruitment or any interview scheduled by the candidate and not the recruiter. That should not prevent the interviewee from seeking to play an equal part in what should be a fair exchange of information. Too often the untutored candidate allows the interview to become one-sided. The employer asks all the questions and the candidate simply responds. The ideal would be for two mutually interested parties to sit down and discuss possibilities for each. This is a conversation of significance, and it requires preparation, thought about the tone of the interview, and planning of the nature and details of the information to be exchanged.

Preparing for the Interview

The length of most initial interviews is about thirty minutes. Given the brevity, the information that is exchanged ought to be important. The candidate should be delivering material that the employer cannot discover on the résumé, and in turn, the candidate should be learning things about the employer that he or she could not otherwise find out. After all, if you have only thirty minutes, why waste time on information that is already published? The information exchanged is more than just factual, and both sides will learn much from what they see of each other, as well. How the candidate looks, speaks, and acts are important to the employer. The employer's attention to the interview and awareness of the candidate's résumé, the setting, and the quality of information presented are important to the candidate.

Just as the employer has every right to be disappointed when a prospect is late for the interview, looks unkempt, and seems ill-prepared to answer fairly standard questions, the candidate may be disappointed with an interviewer who isn't ready for the meeting, hasn't learned the basic résumé facts, and is constantly interrupted by telephone calls. In either situation there's good reason to feel let down.

There are many elements to a successful interview, and some of them are not easy to describe or prepare for. Sometimes there is just a chemistry between interviewer and interviewee that brings out the best in both, and a good exchange takes place. But there is much the candidate can do to pave the way for success in terms of his or her résumé, personal appearance, goals, and interview strategy—each of which we will discuss. However, none of this preparation is as important as the time and thought the candidate gives to personal self-assessment.

Self-Assessment
Neither a stunning résumé nor an expensive, well-tailored suit can compensate for candidates who do not know what they want, where they are going, or why they are interviewing with a particular employer. Self-assessment, the

process by which we begin to know and acknowledge our own particular blend of education, experiences, needs, and goals, is not something that can be sorted out the weekend before a major interview. Of all the elements of interview preparation, this one requires the longest lead time and cannot be faked.

Because the time allotted for most interviews is brief, it is all the more important for job candidates to understand and express succinctly why they are there and what they have to offer. This is not a time for undue modesty (or for braggadocio either); it is a time for a compelling, reasoned statement of why you feel that you and this employer might make a good match. It means you have to have thought about your skills, interests, and attributes; related those to your life experiences and your own history of challenges and opportunities; and determined what that indicates about your strengths, preferences, values, and areas needing further development.

If you need some assistance with self-assessment issues, refer to Chapter 1. Included are suggested exercises that can be done as needed, such as making up an experiential diary and extracting obvious strengths and weaknesses from past experiences. These simple assignments will help you look at past activities as collections of tasks with accompanying skills and responsibilities. Don't overlook your high school or college career office. Many offer personal counseling on self-assessment issues and may provide testing instruments such as the *Myers-Briggs Type Indicator (MBTI)*, the *Harrington-O'Shea Career Decision-Making System (CDM)*, the *Strong Interest Inventory (SII)*, or any other of a wide selection of assessment tools that can help you clarify some of these issues prior to the interview stage of your job search.

The Résumé

Résumé preparation has been discussed in detail, and some basic examples were provided. In this section we want to concentrate on how best to use your résumé in the interview. In most cases the employer will have seen the résumé prior to the interview, and, in fact, it may well have been the quality of that résumé that secured the interview opportunity.

An interview is a conversation, however, and not an exercise in reading. So, if the employer hasn't seen your résumé and you have brought it along to the interview, wait until asked or until the end of the interview to offer it. Otherwise, you may find yourself staring at the back of your résumé and simply answering "yes" and "no" to a series of questions drawn from that document.

Sometimes an interviewer is not prepared and does not know or recall the contents of the résumé and may use the résumé to a greater or lesser degree as a "prompt" during the interview. It is for you to judge what that may indicate about the individual performing the interview or the employer. If your interviewer seems surprised by the scheduled meeting, relies on the résumé to an inordinate degree, and seems otherwise unfamiliar with your background, this lack of preparation for the hiring process could well be a symptom of general management disorganization or may simply be the result of poor planning on the part of one individual. It is your responsibility as a potential employee to be aware of these signals and make your decisions accordingly.

It is perfectly acceptable for you to guide the conversation back to a more interpersonal style by saying, "Ms. Smith, you might be interested in some recent research experience I gained through an internship that is not detailed on my résumé." This strategy may give you an opportunity to convey more information about your strengths and weaknesses and will reengage the direction of your interview.

By all means, bring at least one copy of your résumé to the interview. Occasionally, at the close of an interview, an interviewer will express an interest in circulating a résumé to several departments, and you could then offer the copy you brought. Sometimes, an interview appointment provides an opportunity to meet others in the organization who may express an interest in you and your background, and it may be helpful to follow up with a copy of your résumé. Our best advice, however, is to keep it out of sight until needed or requested.

Employer Information

Whether your interview is for graduate school admission, an overseas corporate position, or a position with a local company, it is important to know something about the employer or the organization. Keeping in mind that the interview is relatively brief and that you will hopefully have other interviews with other organizations, it is important to keep your research in proportion. If secondary interviews are called for, you will have additional time to do further research. For the first interview, it is helpful to know the organization's mission, goals, size, scope of operations, and so forth. Your research may uncover recent areas of challenge or particular successes that may help to fuel the interview. Use the "What Do They Call the Job You Want?" section of Chapter 3, your library, and your career or guidance office to help you locate this information in the most efficient way possible. Don't be shy in asking advice of these counseling and guidance professionals on how best to spend your preparation time. With some practice, you'll soon learn how much information is enough and which kinds of information are most useful to you.

Interview Content

We've already discussed how it can help to think of the interview as an important conversation—one that, as with any conversation, you want to find pleasant and interesting and to leave you with a good feeling. But because this conversation is especially important, the information that's exchanged is critical to its success. What do you want them to know about you? What do you need to know about them? What interview technique do you need to particularly pay attention to? How do you want to manage the close of the interview? What steps will follow in the hiring process?

Except for the professional interviewer, most of us find interviewing stressful and anxiety-provoking. Developing a strategy before you begin interviewing will help you relieve some stress and anxiety. One particular strategy that has worked for many and may work for you is interviewing by objective. Before you interview, write down three to five goals you would like to achieve for that interview. They may be technique goals: Smile a little more, have a firmer handshake, be sure to ask about the next stage in the interview process before leaving. They may be content-oriented goals: Find out about the company's current challenges and opportunities; be sure to speak of your recent research, writing experiences, or foreign travel. Whatever your goals, jot down a few of them as goals for each interview.

Most people find that in trying to achieve these few goals, their interviewing technique becomes more organized and focused. After the interview, the most common question friends and family ask is "How did it go?" With this technique, you have an indication of whether you met *your* goals for the meeting, not just some vague idea of how it went. Chances are, if you accomplished what you wanted to, it improved the quality of the entire interview. As you continue to interview, you will want to revise your goals to continue improving your interview skills.

Now, add to the concept of the significant conversation the idea of a beginning, a middle, and a closing and you will have two thoughts that will give your interview a distinctive character. Be sure to make your introduction warm and cordial. Say your full name (and if it's a difficult-to-pronounce name, help the interviewer to pronounce it) and make certain you know your interviewer's name and how to pronounce it. Most interviews begin with some "soft talk" about the weather, chat about the candidate's trip to the interview site, or national events. This is done as a courtesy to relax both you and the interviewer, to get you talking, and to generally try to defuse the atmosphere of excessive tension. Try to be yourself, engage in the conversation, and don't try to second-guess the interviewer. This is simply what it appears to be—casual conversation.

Once you and the interviewer move on to exchange more serious information in the middle part of the interview, the two most important concerns become your ability to handle challenging questions and your success at asking meaningful ones. Interviewer questions will probably fall into one of three categories: personal assessment and career direction, academic assessment, and knowledge of the employer. Here are a few examples of questions in each category:

Personal Assessment and Career Direction
1. What motivates you to put forth your best effort?
2. What do you consider to be your greatest strengths and weaknesses?
3. What qualifications do you have that make you think you will be successful in this career?

Academic Assessment
1. What led you to choose your major?
2. What subjects did you like best and least? Why?
3. How has your college experience prepared you for this career?

Knowledge of the Employer
1. What do you think it takes to be successful in an organization like ours?
2. In what ways do you think you can make a contribution to our organization?
3. Why did you choose to seek a position with this organization?

The interviewer wants a response to each question but is also gauging your enthusiasm, preparedness, and willingness to communicate. In each response you should provide some information about yourself that can be related to the employer's needs. A common mistake is to give too much information. Answer each question completely, but be careful not to run on too long with extensive details or examples.

Questions About Underdeveloped Skills

Most employers interview people who have met some minimum criteria of education and experience. They interview candidates to see who they are, to learn what kind of personality they exhibit, and to get some sense of how they might fit into the existing organization. It may be that you are asked about skills the employer hopes to find and that you have not documented. Maybe it's grant-writing experience, knowledge of the European political system, or a knowledge of the film world.

To questions about skills and experiences you don't have, answer honestly and forthrightly and try to offer some additional information about skills you do have. For example, perhaps the employer is disappointed you have no grant-writing experience. An honest answer may be as follows:

No, unfortunately, I was never in a position to acquire those skills. I do understand something of the complexities of the grant-writing process and feel confident that my attention to detail, careful reading skills, and strong writing would make grants a wonderful challenge in a new job. I think I could get up on the learning curve quickly.

The employer hears an honest admission of lack of experience but is reassured by some specific skill details that do relate to grant writing and a confident manner that suggests enthusiasm and interest in a challenge.

For many students, questions about their possible contribution to an employer's organization can prove challenging. Because your education has probably not included specific training for a job, you need to review your academic record and select capabilities you have developed in your major that an employer can appreciate. For example, perhaps you read well and can analyze and condense what you've read into smaller, more focused pieces. That could be valuable. Or maybe you did some serious research and you know you have valuable investigative skills. Your public speaking might be highly developed and you might use visual aids appropriately and effectively. Or maybe your skill at correspondence, memos, and messages is effective. Whatever it is, you must take it out of the academic context and put it into a new, employer-friendly context so your interviewer can best judge how you could help the organization.

Exhibiting knowledge of the organization will, without a doubt, show the interviewer that you are interested enough in the available position to have done some legwork in preparation for the interview. Remember, it is not necessary to know every detail of the organization's history but rather to have a general knowledge about why it is in business and how the industry is faring.

Sometime during the interview, generally after the midway point, you'll be asked if you have any questions for the interviewer. Your questions will tell the employer much about your attitude and your desire to understand the organization's expectations so you can compare them to your own strengths. The following are just a few questions you might want to ask:

1. What is the communication style of the organization? (meetings, memos, and so forth)
2. What would a typical day in this position be like for me?
3. What have been some of the interesting challenges and opportunities your organization has recently faced?

Most interviews draw to a natural closing point, so be careful not to prolong the discussion. At a signal from the interviewer, wind up your presentation, express your appreciation for the opportunity, and be sure to ask what the next stage in the process will be. When can you expect to hear from them? Will they be conducting second-tier interviews? If you are interested and haven't heard, would they mind a phone call? Be sure to collect a business card with the name and phone number of your interviewer. On your way out, you might have an opportunity to pick up organizational literature you haven't seen before.

With the right preparation—a thorough self-assessment, professional clothing, and employer information—you'll be able to set and achieve the goals you have established for the interview process.

Interview Follow-Up

Quite often there is a considerable time lag between interviewing for a position and being hired or, in the case of the networker, between your phone call or letter to a possible contact and the opportunity of a meeting. This can be frustrating. "Why aren't they contacting me?" "I thought I'd get another interview, but no one has telephoned." "Am I out of the running?" You don't know what is happening.

Consider the Differing Perspectives
Of course, there is another perspective—that of the networker or hiring organization. Organizations are complex, with multiple tasks that need to be accomplished each day. Hiring is a discrete activity that does not occur as frequently as other job assignments. The hiring process might have to take

second place to other, more immediate organizational needs. Although it may be very important to you, and it is certainly ultimately significant to the employer, other issues such as fiscal management, planning and product development, employer vacation periods, or financial constraints may prevent an organization or individual within that organization from acting on your employment or your request for information as quickly as you or they would prefer.

Use Your Communication Skills

Good communication is essential here to resolve any anxieties, and the responsibility is on you, the job or information seeker. Too many job seekers and networkers offer as an excuse that they don't want to "bother" the organization by writing letters or calling. Let us assure you here and now, once and for all, that if you are troubling an organization by overcommunicating, someone will indicate that situation to you quite clearly. If not, you can only assume you are a worthwhile prospect and the employer appreciates being reminded of your availability and interest. Let's look at follow-up practices in the job interview process and the networking situation separately.

Following Up on the Employment Interview

A brief thank-you note following an interview is an excellent and polite way to begin a series of follow-up communications with a potential employer with whom you have interviewed and want to remain in touch. It should be just that—a thank-you for a good meeting. If you failed to mention some fact or experience during your interview that you think might add to your candidacy, you may use this note to do that. However, this should be essentially a note whose overall tone is appreciative and, if appropriate, indicative of a continuing interest in pursuing any opportunity that may exist with that organization. It is one of the few pieces of business correspondence that may be handwritten, but always use plain, good-quality, standard-size paper.

If, however, at this point you are no longer interested in the employer, the thank-you note is an appropriate time to indicate that. You are under no obligation to identify any reason for not continuing to pursue employment with that organization, but if you are so inclined to indicate your professional reasons (pursuing other employers more akin to your interests, looking for greater income production than this employer can provide, a different geographic location), you certainly may. It should not be written with an eye to negotiation, for it will not be interpreted as such.

As part of your interview closing, you should have taken the initiative to establish lines of communication for continuing information about your candidacy. If you asked permission to telephone, wait a week following your thank-you note, then telephone your contact simply to inquire how things are progressing on your employment status. The feedback you receive here should be taken at face value. If your interviewer simply has no information, he or she will tell you so and indicate whether you should call again and when. Don't be discouraged if this should continue over some period of time.

If during this time something occurs that you think improves or changes your candidacy (some new qualification or experience you may have had), including any offers from other organizations, by all means telephone or write to inform the employer about this. In the case of an offer from a competing but less desirable or equally desirable organization, telephone your contact, explain what has happened, express your real interest in the organization, and inquire whether some determination on your employment might be made before you must respond to this other offer. An organization that is truly interested in you may be moved to make a decision about your candidacy. Equally possible is the scenario in which they are not yet ready to make a decision and so advise you to take the offer that has been presented. Again, you have no ethical alternative but to deal with the information presented in a straightforward manner.

When accepting other employment, be sure to contact any employers still actively considering you and inform them of your new job. Thank them graciously for their consideration. There are many other job seekers out there just like you who will benefit from having their candidacy improved when others bow out of the race. Who knows, you might at some future time have occasion to interact professionally with one of the organizations with which you sought employment. How embarrassing it would be to have someone remember you as the candidate who failed to notify them that you were taking a job elsewhere!

In all of your follow-up communications, keep good notes of whom you spoke with, when you called, and any instructions that were given about return communications. This will prevent any misunderstandings and provide you with good records of what has transpired.

Job Offer Considerations

For many recent college graduates, the thrill of their first job and, for some, the most substantial regular income they have ever earned seems an excess of good fortune coming at once. To question that first income or to be critical in any way of the conditions of employment at the time of the initial offer seems like looking a gift horse in the mouth. It doesn't seem to occur to many new hires even to attempt to negotiate any aspect of their first job. And, as many employers who deal with entry-level jobs for recent college graduates will readily confirm, the reality is that there simply isn't much movement in salary available to these new college recruits. The entry-level hire generally does not have an employment track record on a professional level to provide any leverage for negotiation. Real negotiations on salary, benefits, retirement provisions, and so forth come to those with significant employment records at higher income levels.

Of course, the job offer is more than just money. It can be composed of geographic assignment, duties and responsibilities, training, benefits, health and medical insurance, educational assistance, car allowance or company vehicle, and a host of other items. All of this is generally detailed in the formal letter that presents the final job offer. In most cases this is a follow-up to a personal phone call from the employer representative who has been principally responsible for your hiring process.

That initial telephone offer is certainly binding as a verbal agreement, but most firms follow up with a detailed letter outlining the most significant parts of your employment contract. You may, of course, choose to respond immediately at the time of the telephone offer (which would be considered a binding oral contract), but you will also be required to formally answer the letter of offer with a letter of acceptance, restating the salient elements of the employer's description of your position, salary, and benefits. This ensures that both parties are clear on the terms and conditions of employment and remuneration and any other outstanding aspects of the job offer.

Is This the Job You Want?

Most new employees will respond affirmatively in writing, glad to be in the position to accept employment. If you've worked hard to get the offer and the job market is tight, other offers may not be in sight, so you will say, "Yes, I accept!" What is important here is that the job offer you accept be one that does fit your particular needs, values, and interests as you've outlined them in your self-assessment process. Moreover, it should be a job that will not only use your skills and education but also challenge you to develop new skills and talents.

Jobs are sometimes accepted too hastily, for the wrong reasons, and without proper scrutiny by the applicant. For example, an individual might readily accept a sales job only to find the continual rejection by potential clients unendurable. An office worker might realize within weeks the constraints of a desk job and yearn for more activity. Employment is an important part of our lives. It is, for most of our adult lives, our most continuous productive activity. We want to make good choices based on the right criteria.

If you have a low tolerance for risk, a job based on commission will certainly be very anxiety-provoking. If being near your family is important, issues of relocation could present a decision crisis for you. If you're an adventurous person, a job with frequent travel would provide needed excitement and be very desirable. The importance of income, the need to continue your education, your personal health situation—all of these have an impact on whether the job you are considering will ultimately meet your needs. Unless you've spent some time understanding and thinking about these issues, it will be difficult to evaluate offers you do receive.

More important, if you make a decision that you cannot tolerate and feel you must leave that job, you will then have both unemployment and self-esteem issues to contend with. These will combine to make the next job search tough going, indeed. So make your acceptance a carefully considered decision.

Negotiate Your Offer

It may be that there is some aspect of your job offer that is not particularly attractive to you. Perhaps there is no relocation allotment to help you move your possessions, and this presents some financial hardship for you. It may be that the health insurance is less than you had hoped. Your initial assignment may be different from what you expected, either in its location or in the duties and responsibilities that comprise it. Or it may simply be that the salary is less than you anticipated. Other considerations may be your official starting date of employment, vacation time, evening hours, dates of training programs or schools, and other concerns.

If you are considering not accepting the job because of some item or items in the job offer "package" that do not meet your needs, you should know that most employers emphatically wish that you would bring that issue to their attention. It may be that the employer can alter it to make the offer more agreeable for you. In some cases it cannot be changed. In any event the employer would generally like to have the opportunity to try to remedy a difficulty rather than risk losing a good potential employee over an issue that might have been resolved. After all, they have spent time and funds in securing your services, and they certainly deserve an opportunity to resolve any possible differences.

Honesty is the best approach in discussing any objections or uneasiness you might have over the employer's offer. Having received your formal offer in writing, contact your employer representative and indicate your particular dissatisfaction in a straightforward manner. For example, you might explain that while you are very interested in being employed by this organization, the salary (or any other benefit) is less than you have determined you require. State the terms you need, and listen to the response. You may be asked to put this in writing, or you may be asked to hold off until the firm can decide on a response. If you are dealing with a senior representative of the organization, one who has been involved in hiring for some time, you may get an immediate response or a solid indication of possible outcomes.

Perhaps the issue is one of relocation. Your initial assignment is in the Midwest, and because you had indicated a strong West Coast preference, you are surprised at the actual assignment. You might simply indicate that while you understand the need for the company to assign you based on its needs, you are disappointed and had hoped to be placed on the West Coast. You could inquire if that were still possible and, if not, would it be reasonable to expect a West Coast relocation in the future.

If your request is presented in a reasonable way, most employers will not see this as jeopardizing your offer. If they can agree to your proposal, they will. If not, they will simply tell you so, and you may choose to continue your candidacy with them or remove yourself from consideration. The choice will be up to you.

Some firms will adjust benefits within their parameters to meet the candidate's need if at all possible. If a candidate requires a relocation cost allowance, he or she may be asked to forgo tuition benefits for the first year to accomplish this adjustment. An increase in life insurance may be adjusted by some other benefit trade-off; perhaps a family dental plan is not needed. In these decisions you are called upon, sometimes under time pressure, to know how you value these issues and how important each is to you.

Many employers find they are more comfortable negotiating for candidates who have unique qualifications or who bring especially needed expertise to the organization. Employers hiring large numbers of entry-level college graduates may be far more reluctant to accommodate any changes in offer conditions. They are well supplied with candidates with similar education and experience so that if rejected by one candidate, they can draw new candidates from an ample labor pool.

Compare Offers

The condition of the economy, the job seeker's academic major and particular geographic job market, and individual needs and demands for certain employment conditions may not provide more than one job offer at a time. Some job seekers may feel that no reasonable offer should go unaccepted for the simple fear there won't be another.

In a tough job market, or if the job you seek is not widely available, or when your job search goes on too long and becomes difficult to sustain financially and emotionally, it may be necessary to accept an inferior offer. The alternative is continued unemployment. Even here, when you feel you don't have a choice, you can at least understand that in accepting this particular offer, there may be limitations and conditions you don't appreciate. At the time of acceptance, there were no other alternatives, but you can begin to use that position to gain the experience and talent to move toward a more attractive position.

Sometimes, however, more than one offer is received, and the candidate has the luxury of choice. If the job seeker knows what he or she wants and has done the necessary self-assessment honestly and thoroughly, it may be clear that one of the offers conforms more closely to those expressed wants and needs.

However, if, as so often happens, the offers are similar in terms of conditions and salary, the question then becomes which organization might provide the necessary climate, opportunities, and advantages for your professional development and growth. This is the time when solid employer research and astute questioning during the interviews really pay off. How much did you learn about the employer through your own research and skillful questioning? When the interviewer asked during the interview "Do you have any questions?" did you ask the kinds of questions that would help resolve a choice between one organization and another? Just as an employer must decide among numerous applicants, so must the applicant learn to assess the potential employer. Both are partners in the job search.

Reneging on an Offer

An especially disturbing occurrence for employers and career counseling professionals is when a job seeker formally (either orally or by written contract) accepts employment with one organization and later reneges on the agreement and goes with another employer.

There are all kinds of rationalizations offered for this unethical behavior. None of them satisfies. The sad irony is that what the job seeker is willing to do to the employer—make a promise and then break it—he or she would be outraged to have done to him- or herself: have the job offer pulled. It is a very bad way to begin a career. It suggests the individual has not taken the time to do the necessary self-assessment and self-awareness exercises to think and judge critically. The new offer taken may, in fact, be no better or worse than the one refused. You should be aware that there have been incidents of legal action following job candidates' reneging on an offer. This adds a very sour note to what should be a harmonious beginning of a lifelong adventure.

PART TWO

THE CAREER PATHS

5

Introduction to Geology Career Paths

Geology is one of the most fascinating career areas in which to be employed. To unravel just a small part of the mysteries of this earth provides an enormous amount of satisfaction for those working in this field. So what is the mystery and mystique all about? This chapter discusses the general field of geology to give you a taste of what you can expect when you enter this exciting and challenging field.

Geologists, also known as geological scientists or geoscientists, study the physical aspects and history of our planet. They identify and examine rocks, collect data via remote sensing instruments such as satellites, conduct geological surveys, construct field maps, and use instruments to measure the Earth's gravity and magnetic field. They also analyze information collected through seismic studies, which involves bouncing energy waves off buried rock layers. Many geologists and geophysicists search for oil, natural gas, minerals, and groundwater, and they examine the chemical and physical properties of specimens in laboratories. In addition, both geologists and geophysicists may study the fossil remains of animal and plant life, or experiment with the flow of water and oil through rocks.

What is the difference between geologists, geophysicists, and geoscientists? These persons work in closely related fields, but there are major differences in the work they do. Geologists study the composition, structure, and history of the Earth's crust. They try to find out how rocks were formed and what has happened to them since formation. Geophysicists use the principles of physics, mathematics, and chemistry to study not only the Earth's surface, but also its internal composition; ground and surface waters; atmosphere; oceans; and its magnetic, electrical, and gravitational forces. Both geologists and geophysicists commonly apply their skills and knowledge to the search for natural resources and the solution of environmental problems. Geoscientists are educated and skilled in both geology and geophysics. For the most part, however, we will use the word "geologist" as a general term to avoid confusion.

Technology in Geology

Technology has played a considerable part in moving the science of geology forward; today's geologist must be comfortable with and adept at using the latest computer programs and high-tech tools. For example, geologists use two- or three-dimensional computer modeling to portray water layers and the flow of water or other fluids through rock cracks and porous materials. They also use computer simulations that replicate the Earth's magnetic fields, providing new insights into the geology, lithospheric structure, and tectonic evolution below the ice in Antarctica. Geologists rely on a variety of sophisticated laboratory instruments, including x-ray diffractometers, which determine the crystal structure of minerals, and petrographic microscopes, for the study of rock and sediment samples. Geoscientists work with seismographs, instruments that measure energy waves resulting from movements in the Earth's crust, to determine the locations and intensities of earthquakes.

Geoscientists working in metal mining or the oil and gas industries sometimes process and interpret the maps produced by remote sensing satellites to help identify potential new mineral, oil, or gas deposits. Seismic technology also is an important exploration tool. Seismic waves are used to develop three-dimensional computer models of underground or underwater rock formations. Seismic reflection technology may also reveal unusual underground features that sometimes indicate accumulations of natural gas or petroleum, facilitating exploration and reducing the risks associated with drilling in previously unexplored areas.

The Training You'll Need

A bachelor's degree in geology or geophysics is adequate for entry-level jobs, but better jobs with good advancement potential usually require at least a master's degree in geology or geophysics. The higher the degree you earn, the more specialized you will become in one particular subscience of geology.

A bachelor's degree will give you a broad, basic understanding of geologic processes. Government agencies, such as departments of transportation or environmental protection agencies, or companies that provide environmental consulting often want people with an elementary understanding of geology for studying local problems, collecting environmental samples, or supervising drilling or surveys.

Many geology careers require, at a minimum, a master's degree in order for applicants to be considered for positions. In particular, government jobs and those with private firms often prefer to hire candidates with a master's degree. A geologist holding a master's degree will still have studied general geology, but will also be an "expert" in a specialized subfield such as geochemistry or hydrogeology. With a graduate degree and a particular specialization, you may have to relocate to other parts of the country or even to other countries. This is particularly true if you want to advance in a large national or international business or if you want to work in an academic setting.

Most research and teaching positions in colleges and universities, federal agencies, and some state geological surveys involving basic research require candidates to have a Ph.D. Industries such as the petroleum or mining industries or larger engineering firms hire Ph.D.s for their research divisions and for specializations in engineering geology, economic geology, and hydrogeology. Greater advancement opportunities and expertise in the field can be gained through the advanced study and research required to achieve a Ph.D.

Traditional geoscience courses emphasizing classical geologic methods and topics (such as mineralogy, paleontology, stratigraphy, and structural geology) are important for all geoscientists, however, some fields require specific areas of study. If you are interested in working in the environmental or regulatory fields, for example, either in environmental consulting firms or for the federal or a state government, you should take more specialized courses in hydrology, hazardous waste management, environmental legislation, chemistry, fluid mechanics, and geologic logging. On the other hand, if you are planning on working in the mining or oil and gas extraction industries, you should gain an understanding of environmental regulations and government permit issues during your studies.

Computer skills are essential for all prospective geoscientists. In school, you should gain some experience with computer modeling, data analysis and integration, digital mapping, remote sensing, and geographic information systems (GIS). In general, you should be comfortable with new technologies in order to work and excel in any number of geology careers.

Some employers seek applicants with field experience, so it may benefit you to obtain a summer internship. This kind of work allows you to make contacts in the field and gain some first-hand knowledge of the kind of work you'll be doing after you graduate. Having experience in an internship also allows you to build your résumé.

Choosing Your Path

During your undergraduate program it is important to consider where your studies will take you. Do you want to find work with your bachelor's degree or go on for graduate studies? Would you prefer to work in private industry (oil, coal, gas, mining, and environmental consulting companies), for the government, or for a university as a teacher or researcher?

Initially, it's best if you remain flexible; do not become too narrowly focused early on in your education, giving emphasis to one area to the exclusion of others. Though you may gain expertise in one field, later you may be drawn into another field entirely. Many geoscientists find that their interests shift; a geochemist may become concerned with paleontological problems. A geophysicist may become involved in structural geology. An economic geologist may focus on environmental matters. There are so many options that the more exposure you allow yourself, the more satisfied you'll be with your choice.

You may wish to combine a degree in the geosciences with another area of expertise, such as secondary education, technical writing, sales of technological or scientific equipment, business management, or public relations in geology-related industries. An advantage to these geology-related careers is that the requirements for employment are often satisfied with a bachelor's degree, as opposed to many technically oriented careers, which usually require the completion of a master's degree in geology. Keeping an open mind and understanding your interests and talents may lead you into any number of interesting directions with your geology degree.

Jobs for Geology Majors

Traditionally, geologists have found jobs in government, higher education, the petroleum industry, or the mining industry. Today even more options exist as the growing awareness of the need for geologic information in engineering and environmental protection develops. Government agencies, such as state geological surveys, water resource divisions, and departments of transportation are viable areas for employment. Private industry engineering firms, including the geotechnical engineering firms and firms that deal with the legal aspects of environmental problems, also are hiring.

Geologists hold about 101,000 jobs nationwide as environmental geologists and geoscientists; this does not include those working in colleges and universities. According to government statistics, about 47 percent of environmental geologists working today are employed by state and local governments; 14 percent work in architectural, engineering, and related fields; 13 percent in management, scientific, and technical consulting service; and 9 percent are employed by the federal government. Among geoscientists, 30 percent were employed in architectural, engineering, and related services, and 15 percent worked for oil and gas extraction companies. The federal government employs about 3,000 geoscientists, including geologists, geophysicists, and oceanographers, mostly within the U.S. Department of the Interior (doi.gov) for the U.S. Geological Survey (USGS; usgs.gov) and within the U.S. Department of Defense (defenselink.mil). Another 3,400 work for state agencies, such as state geological surveys and state Departments of Conservation.

Geologists work in a variety of different settings. Some spend the majority of their time in an office or classroom, but many others divide their time between fieldwork and office or laboratory work. Geologists often travel to remote sites by helicopter or four-wheel-drive vehicles and cover large areas on foot. For example, exploration geologists and geophysicists often work overseas or in isolated areas, while marine geologists and oceanographers may spend considerable time at sea on academic research ships.

In order to protect the public and the environment, most states require those working as geologists to register with the state, take a standardized test, and receive a license to practice. To become registered you must pass the state registration exam to demonstrate a basic knowledge of geology. Review the state board website of the state in which you live for more detailed information about this process.

The following alphabetical list is a representative sample of current—and very diverse—job titles that can be held by geology majors. As you'll see, these titles span a range of fields and areas of expertise. Having a double major in such diverse areas as geology and photography, for example, may lead to an exciting career in aerial photography!

Agricultural engineer
Architect
Astronomer
Cartographer
Computer analyst
Cooperative extension agent
Economic geologist
Environmental consultant
Environmental lawyer
Geodynamacist
Geologist project manager
Geophysics technician
Geotechnical engineer
Glacial geologist
Industrial hygienist
Instrumentation technician

Laboratory technician
Landscape/nursery manager
Marine advisor
Materials analyst
Mathematician
Medical doctor
Meteorologist
Mineralogist
Mining engineer
Oceanographer
Paleoceanographer
Paleoclimatologist
Park naturalist
Parks and natural resource manager
Peace Corps worker
Petroleum engineer
Petrologist
Planetary geologist
Pollution control specialist
Pollution remediator
Prospector
Sales engineer
Sedimentologist
Soil scientist
Stratigrapher
Structural geologist
Surveyor
Technical writer/communicator
Urban/regional planner
Volcanologist
Waste management specialist
Water quality control technician
Water remote sensing interpreter
Well logging specialist

Career Outlooks for Geologists

According to government statistics, the overall employment of environmental scientists and geoscientists is expected to grow about as fast as the average for all occupations through 2012, although employment growth does vary by specialty. Public policy, forcing companies and organizations to comply with environmental laws and regulations, particularly those regarding groundwater contamination, clean air, and flood control, will drive job growth in the government sectors and in the environmental fields. A general heightened awareness regarding the need to monitor the quality of the environment, to interpret the impact of human actions on terrestrial and aquatic ecosystems, and to develop strategies for ecosystem restoration are all increasingly important issues that will drive demand for environmental scientists. Issues related to water conservation, deteriorating coastal environments, and rising sea levels also will stimulate employment growth of these workers. As the population increases and moves to more environmentally sensitive locations, environmental scientists will be needed to assess building sites for potential geologic hazards, to mitigate the effects of natural hazards such as floods, tornadoes, and earthquakes, and to address issues related to pollution control and waste disposal. Organizations and governments will also need these workers to conduct research on hazardous-waste sites in order to determine the impact of hazardous pollutants on soil and groundwater so that engineers can design remediation systems.

In the past, employment of geologists and some other geoscientists has been cyclical and largely affected by the price of oil and gas. When prices were low, oil and gas producers curtailed exploration activities and laid off geologists. When prices were higher, companies had the funds and incentive to renew exploration efforts and hire geoscientists in large numbers. In recent years, a growing worldwide demand for oil and gas and for new exploration and recovery techniques—particularly in deep water and previously inaccessible sites—has returned a modicum of stability to the petroleum industry. Growth in this area might be limited by the increasing efficiencies in finding oil and gas. Geoscientists who speak a foreign language and who are willing to work abroad should, however, find ample employment opportunities. An expected increase in highway building and repair of older highways and other infrastructure projects will be another good source of jobs for engineering geologists. In general, jobs for geologists should be available in every area of specialty.

Strategies for Finding Jobs

There are a variety of strategies you can employ to help you land your first geology job, whether you're still in school or you've graduated. This section presents a brief discussion of some of these techniques and sources of information for finding jobs. For more detailed information, there are a variety of job hunting and résumé books available. Use an online bookseller to search the titles for one specific to your needs. In addition, see Appendix B for websites pertinent to job hunting.

College Career Placement Centers

College placement or resource centers are excellent sources of information. The staff is made up of experts in finding and applying for jobs and, since they're employed by the university, their focus is on helping students like you create a résumé and locate jobs. Check in with a career counselor regularly to see what opportunities are available. Career offices regularly receive mailings of job openings and usually have good insider information about summer jobs and internships. You can also create a résumé and obtain letters of recommendation and keep them on file in the office.

Help Wanted Ads

Statistics show that between 5.5 and 14 percent of job seekers get their jobs from help wanted ads, a fairly low number of overall applicants. This means that competition for jobs advertised in papers is keen and many people obtain their jobs from other sources. Still, you should regularly peruse the newspapers in your area or in the geographic location in which you would prefer to work in order to get a idea of the availability of jobs. Additionally, you may find a related job in a company that may have other opportunities. Calling the human resources departments of such companies may yield other opportunities not yet made available to the public. Finally, a trip to the library will reveal periodicals you might not have been aware of, especially those in other geographic areas if you're considering moving; using the library will be less of a burden on your budget.

The Internet

The Internet is an incredible source for job hunting—just take a look at Appendix B! A keyword search using any of the search engines available to you will yield a variety of jobs. Keep your search specific in order to narrow down the numbers of relevant results. For example, if you want to work as an environmental geologist in Texas, use the keywords "job environmental geologist Texas." You will discover a wealth of information online—professional associations with job banks and job placement services; educational institutions listing their job openings; professional publications such as newsletters and journals, with job listings; and a wide variety of potential employers and job search services—most of which are available to you at no charge.

Internships and Networking

Internships are important keys to finding work in many different settings. These jobs allow you to break into the field and gain some hands-on experience. They give you the chance to see firsthand what the work is like so you can make a more educated decision about your future in the field. Also, internships often lead to jobs because you'll be able to prove yourself to a prospective employer and network with those in the field.

Networking is the way most people find the best jobs. Networking simply means that you talk to people in the field, query them about their skills and experience, and let them know you're interested in positions if they become available. Most people working in the field would be happy to share their experience and advice with an enthusiastic student, so don't be afraid to ask for informational interviews—just be sure to leave them with your contact information so that they can let you know if they hear of any openings!

Associations and Organizations

Industry associations and organizations are valuable sources of information about jobs pertinent to your field or area of interest. Many associations also have their own journal, which often features more targeted help wanted ads. For example, the *Chronicle of Higher Education* (http://chronicle.com) is the old standby for those seeking positions within colleges and universities. Check out the website to find out more information about this organization and publication and Appendix A for a list of various other organizations. More information can also be found doing keyword searches for organizations and associations not listed in the appendix.

The following chapters present a bevy of geology careers, loosely organized by focus of study. If you read something that piques your interest, do an online search to find out more information about the kind of work the job entails. You may also wish to use the resources in Appendix A to gather more information. Finally, Appendix B has job search websites, both general and geology specific, that you can use to find the job of your dreams. Good luck!

6

Path I: Oil and Gas, Minerals and Mining

Oil and natural gas furnish about three-fifths of our energy needs, fueling our homes, workplaces, factories, and transportation systems. In addition, they constitute the raw materials for plastics, chemicals, medicines, fertilizers, and synthetic fibers. Petroleum, commonly referred to as oil, is a natural fuel formed from the decay of plants and animals buried beneath the ground, under tremendous heat and pressure, for millions of years. Formed by a similar process, natural gas often is found in separate deposits and is sometimes mixed with oil. Finding, developing, and extracting oil and gas are the primary functions of the oil and gas extraction industry and the focus of many different kinds of workers in this field, including petroleum geologists.

Mineral resources have played an important role in the development of many countries, including the United States. Efficient, environmentally sound production of mineral resources will continue as a major factor in our economy for the foreseeable future. Mineral deposits occur in all rock types, in all geological settings, and in rocks of all ages. In particular, North America is a major producer of iron, nickel, copper, uranium, zinc, lead, gold, silver, lithium, niobium, and the rare-earth metals (platinum and palladium), as well as many other by-product metals. Research into the discovery of new sites of these resources and the production of existing sites are necessary to keep the United States at the forefront internationally as a supplier of all types of commodities; this is where jobs in minerals and mining fit in.

Many jobs for geologists and geophysicists are in or related to the petroleum and mining industries, especially the exploration for oil, gas, metals, and minerals. The mining and the oil and gas industries are sometimes grouped together as one industry. In the late 1970s many oil and gas companies dabbled or were heavily involved in minerals and mining, mainly because of excessive financial reserves earned as a result of the high prices of oil at that time. But now, most oil and gas companies have removed themselves from the mining field altogether. This chapter explores jobs in the petroleum and oil and mineral and mining industries.

Petroleum Geologists

Petroleum geologists study both the origins of hydrocarbon accumulations within the Earth's subsurface as well as current levels of accumulations. Crude oil and natural gas are complexes of hydrogen and carbon, generated through the decomposition of plant and animal remains under heat and pressure. Like coal, their ultimate origin goes back through photosynthesis to solar energy. The source of hydrocarbons is usually an organic-rich shale from which light liquids or gases are expelled and migrate upward. Eventually they are trapped by an impervious layer and accumulate in a reservoir, such as a porous sandstone or limestone. Globally, the greatest production of oil is from young sedimentary rocks, with about 60 percent of production from rocks that are less than 60 million years old.

Petroleum geology uses aerial photographs, fieldwork, well log data, and other tools to understand and determine where accumulations of oil or gas can be found. This type of geologist works with a team to discover likely deposits of oil and gas, and these geologists are often front and center when a new discovery is made. Standing on an oil rig when the drill bit penetrates the ground and finds a new discovery of oil or gas is an exhilarating experience for many of these workers.

A production/development/exploitation geologist creates or refines the process of procuring oil or gas after the discovery. He or she comes in after the discovery is made and conducts the detailed work to determine the specific characteristics of the geology, how many wells will have to be drilled, where they should be drilled, and so forth. This person creates detailed maps and plans strategies for the production of oil or gas after the discovery, working closely with the petroleum engineers to determine the best mode for efficient and cost-effective production.

Training and Education

The foundation of study for petroleum geologists focuses on the geosciences; courses include reservoir geology, seismic principals, applied geophysics, organic geochemistry, plate tectonics, global geology, and petrology, just to name a few. Additionally, petroleum geologists must have a strong math background, in particular, focusing on geostatistics, applied math, algebra, and calculus. Graduates must also have a firm knowledge of computer modeling, including geoscientific systems, geophysical modeling systems, exploration and mapping packages, remote sensing programs, and geophysics processing programs, in addition to the Global Positioning System (GPS), all of which are used to locate new oil and gas fields or pinpoint hidden deposits in existing fields. Other helpful courses include business, economics, finance, and project management.

It takes considerable expertise to locate petroleum, and the petroleum geologist must be well versed in the various branches of petroleum geology, namely, stratigraphy, sedimentology, structural geology, and geophysical techniques. Some of this will be covered in courses either in undergraduate or graduate school or by keeping abreast of the latest industry news from trade magazines or journals. In other cases, you may end up receiving additional training through industry courses. Specific training is often required in order for a geoscientist to become a profitable contributor to his or her company. This type of training is usually obtained after a college or university education. While colleges and universities provide a solid foundational education in geology, specific training is normally provided by an employer, such as a major oil company, as part of a career development program.

For example, Exxon has an initial two-year, extensive work-related training program for newly hired employees. During this period of time, a geologist will work in as many as four different areas of the company, including exploration, production, processing, and planning. The new employee receives special projects designed to give her or him experience is a variety of areas. These projects are supplemented by both internal and external courses and seminars focusing on the area of the assignment.

Lifelong education is a requirement in this field, especially since technological advances are rapid. The American Association of Petroleum Geologists or AAPG (aapg.org) oversees seven training centers worldwide to assist geologists in brushing up on technological and scientific advances. Industry seminars and conventions offer additional opportunities for participating in lectures and discussions.

Employers look for a variety of skills and attributes in their prospective employees, some of which may surprise you. A recent survey conducted by the AAPG showed that written communication, spatial cognitive skills, self-confidence, research skills, conceptualization, and leadership skills were the most prized by employers, followed by entrepreneurial flair, intellectual ability, cultural awareness, and language skills. You should be able to demonstrate these skills either in the form of your résumé or during the interview.

Possible Employers

Employers of petroleum geologists include major oil companies and hundreds of smaller, independent oil exploration, production, and service companies. Because petroleum geologists specialize in the discovery and production of oil and gas, relatively few are employed in the refining, transportation, or retail sectors of the oil and gas industry.

In terms of locale, most petroleum geologists work where oil and gas are found. Large numbers are employed in Texas, Oklahoma, Louisiana, and California, including offshore sites. Also, many American petroleum engineers work overseas in oil-producing countries.

There are opportunities for employment in both large and small companies. In general, however, large companies expect their newly hired employees to possess more technical and nontechnical skills than do their smaller counterparts. Similarly, larger companies look for candidates who have, at minimum, a master's degree. It is generally harder for inexperienced, new graduates to find jobs with smaller companies, whereas larger companies are more open to hiring and training career starters.

Career Outlook

The oil and gas industry, as you might expect, is subject to cyclical fluctuations. During the 1980s and the early 1990s, low oil prices, higher production costs, improvements in energy efficiency, shrinking oil reserves, and restrictions on potential drilling sites caused exploration activities to be curtailed in the United States; this limited the number of job openings for geoscientists in the petroleum and related industries. More recently, a growing worldwide demand for oil and gas, higher prices, and new exploration and recovery techniques, have returned stability to the petroleum industry and increased the demand for these workers.

Growing populations, stronger economies in the United States and abroad, and continuing industrialization of developing countries are driving the need for more energy. At the same time, the oil and gas and related industries—such as petroleum engineering services—are taking advantage of new technologies that lower costs and facilitate exploration and recovery of natural gas and oil, particularly in deep water and other previously inaccessible sites. Because of the lower number of geology degrees awarded in recent years and the significant number of geoscientists who left the industry during earlier periods of downsizing, job opportunities in the petroleum and related industries are expected to continue to be good in the next several years.

Salary and Compensation

As the demand for oil and gas rises, so does the demand for the skills and expertise of petroleum geologists, which means that companies are willing to offer higher salaries to attract qualified persons. In recent years there has been an increase in salaries for petroleum geologists. A 2005 salary survey by the AAPG showed that geologists with zero to two years of experience average $67,800 in salary annually, which is up slightly from the previous year; those with three to five years' experience averaged $75,600 annually, 10.4 percent higher than the previous year; geologists with six to nine years average $77,500, up slightly from the previous year; those with fifteen to nineteen years' experience were up 11.6 percent at an average of $116,000 annually; and geologists with more than 20 years' experience averaged $123,600 annually, a raise of 4.7 percent over the previous year.

Those with higher degrees are able to command higher salaries. The same AAPG survey showed that petroleum geologists with a Bachelor of Science degree and zero to two years of experience earned $62,000 a year, while master's degree holders with the same amount of experience earned $67,100 on average, and those with Ph.D.s earned about $80,000 a year. The same trend can be seen for increasing levels of experience.

Many petroleum geologists also enjoy the benefits of a bonus, which may be a substantial sum of money. Increasingly, companies are using the bonus plan as a major factor in compensation. A bonus plan rewards employees' performance with compensation in addition to their salary. One industry report noted that one company gave top performers bonuses of over 50 percent of their salaries, although this is not the standard industry percentage for bonuses. Signing bonuses for new hires also are common, especially now that demand for petroleum geologists is high.

Mining Geologists

Mining geologists find, extract, and prepare metals and minerals for manufacturing industries. Some mining geologists work with metallurgical engineers to locate and appraise new ore deposits. They may work closely with engineers on the design of open-pit and underground mines, including mineshafts and tunnels in underground operations. These geologists also assist environmental departments with a range of issues—from safety of working conditions to estimating the production potential of the mine from its inception to the end of its productivity.

Mining geologists at the large, open-pit mines are responsible for providing a variety of geological information throughout the life of the mine. Geologists working with producing mines spend much of their time trying to learn about the grade of the mineral or metal, mineralogy, and character of rock in the ground. To do this, they gather and interpret geological data from drill holes and computerized mapping.

Mine geologists examine cuttings from blast holes (spaced about every twenty fife to thirty feet in large mines) and note the rock type, mineralogy, and hydrothermal alteration of the sample. This information is then transferred to maps and transmitted to the ore control department. The geological information is merged with assay data and used to determine what material has the characteristics of ore to be milled, concentrated, and smelted, or leached and recovered. The geological data are compiled, digitized, and incorporated into a short-range geological model used to plan for mining over several months.

Geologists involved with gathering and interpreting data for mid- to long-range planning are often referred to as "project geologists." The typical project involves planning and implementing a plan for drilling, mapping, and compiling earlier data to be able to complete a three-dimensional geological model of a mineral deposit. The raw data are then compiled into a database with geological codes and plotted on cross sections to map the area to be mined.

Mining and minerals geologists use a large variety of sophisticated laboratory instruments, including x-ray diffractometers, which determine the crystal structure of minerals, and petrographic microscopes, for the study of rock and sediment samples. They use sophisticated computer software to determine and map the potential mine and to calculate the yield of the mine. As in most areas of geology, newer and more advanced technology is continually being developed.

Mine geologists are like explorers, continually seeking new mineral deposits. The surest way to do this is to explore areas outside of a known mine or by drilling deeper within the same mine. Geologists develop drill targets they expect should be mineralized and test these spots with drill holes. In this way, geologists keep expanding their knowledge of the deposit and extend the life of the mine. As they gather new data, they build larger and more comprehensive models of the deposit.

Geologists working on mines, especially if they are in the process of drilling and excavating, may end up working long hours, typically five days a week, 10- to 11-hours a day, with some work on weekends. There are, of course, many variables to this, depending on the age and stage of excavation of the mine. The reality for most geologists is long workdays.

Training and Education

Some college courses for mining and mineral geologists, including the basic science and math courses, are the same as for other geological disciplines.

After these prerequisites are obtained, those who wish to focus on the mining and mineral area will be required to take courses in practical geostatistics, modeling and spatial analysis, quality control of geochemical and assay samples, surface geologic data, underground geologic data and reserve estimation, and common rocks and minerals.

Students enrolled in bachelor's or master's degree programs should seek out summer internships to gain experience in the field. Every year there are a limited number of summer internship opportunities available with various companies, both domestic and abroad, working as geological or geophysical field assistants. These jobs provide an excellent way to make industry contacts and build experience.

As in the oil and petroleum industry, new graduates working in the mineral and mining industry are taught skills on the job that relate to specific projects. Mine geologists learn the practical aspects of how a mine site operates while they are on the job, although they may attend courses and conferences to keep their skills up to date. As the new employee puts in more time on the job and gains more experience, responsibilities and supervisory roles increase and the work assigned becomes more diverse, both technically and geographically.

As in other areas, applicants with master's degrees are most widely sought by companies in this industry, although people with bachelor's and doctoral degrees are also able to find employment in lower paying jobs and academia, respectively. Employers also look for strong field experience and professional communication skills, especially the ability to prepare and deliver concise and accurate reports. Foreign language skills and a willingness to work and live internationally are of increasing value to employers.

Possible Employers

Mining companies are the largest employers, however, there are positions in federal and state agencies and some jobs with financial analysts.

A typical career path for a new geology graduate might include spending time mapping and working away from urban settings. Frequently, this work can take the geologist to remote regions, in mountainous or desert terrain, on location at mining or drilling sites, even to hot springs located on the ocean floor.

Mining and minerals geologists often find challenging positions overseas working for foreign governments or mining companies. These positions usually offer attractive salaries and benefits, including housing and free transportation, and often tax-free status. Living conditions, however, can often be primitive, in remote areas, and in regions of political unrest. For example, an exploration geologist with ten years' experience may find lucrative work overseeing a base and precious metals exploration program in an arid terrain in the Middle East.

Companies often seek those with expertise in a particular area. For example, you may find work as a specialist diamond exploration geologist heading a team of exploration geologists in the evaluation of known alluvial diamond resources, along with the exploration for further alluvial and hard-rock diamond occurrences in a developing part of southern Africa.

Career Outlook

Opportunities in the mining industry are closely related to the price of the metals and minerals they produce. If the price of these products is high, it is worthwhile for a mining company to invest millions of dollars in material moving equipment and ore processing technology necessary to operate the mine and make a profit. Today, metal commodities are in demand, thus there are expanding employment opportunities. Although the long-term business environment for mining generally is perceived to be favorable, a mine takes years of research, planning, and development to become fully operational, and even then may not contribute to rapid expansion in employment opportunities for mining engineers.

Many of the available jobs in the United States are temporary, as companies go through big, but short-lived drilling programs. However, due to the relatively low numbers of qualified workers in this area, opportunities should remain good in the future as more experienced mining geologists retire. The outlook in South America and Africa is somewhat better than in the United States, although living and working in these countries can be difficult, especially for workers with families. In general, mining geologists who speak a foreign language and who are willing to work abroad should enjoy the best opportunities, as the need for energy, construction materials, and a broad range of geological expertise grows in developing nations.

Salary and Compensation

The mineral and mining industries are vulnerable to recessions and to changes in prices, among other factors, and usually release workers when exploration and drilling slow down. Consequently, they offer higher salaries, but less job security, than other industries.

A starting geologist can expect to earn $38,500 to $40,000 per year plus benefits, with a mining company. Temporary geologists with mining companies with some experience can expect $150 to $200 per day, with no benefits. Project geologists with experience and senior geologists can expect to make from $53,400 to $65,400. Chief geologists can make from $80,000 to as high as $102,300 a year.

Industry Consultants

In this chapter we have discussed the types of jobs for geologists working for companies in the petroleum and gas and mining and minerals industries. This section describes opportunities for those who wish to be their own boss: industry consultants.

Industry consultants choose the hours they will work and decide what projects they will or will not undertake, although days are often long (ten to twelve hours and longer). The nature of the job is very independent and requires a substantial amount of drive and determination. Many consultants work from home, although they may also have a small office that they lease. This type of independent work can be very stressful because there is no guaranteed or regular paycheck and the success of the venture rests on the consultant's shoulders. That said, those with fortitude and confidence can be very successful in this lucrative area, especially now that there's a demand for geologists' skills.

Mining and petroleum industry consultants provide a range of services, including project evaluation, mining engineering, feasibility studies, project management, conceptual design, and environmental permitting services. Mining consultants and contractors are used more frequently for short-term projects that require special expertise. Petroleum or oil geologists working as consultants generally focus on one geographical area at a time. For example, you may work as a consultant for companies interested in exploring the Permian Basin, which includes part of west Texas and southeastern New Mexico. A consultant may focus on finding areas that are underdeveloped for oil and gas or examining formations that have not been adequately tested for the presence of oil and gas. Consultants may work with partners leasing areas with potential and promoting the prospects in industry partners. Much of the work of a petroleum consultant is similar to that of a geologist employed by a single company; they run correlations of well logs, sample (well cuttings) analyses, and compilations of cross sections and maps using a variety of computer programs.

Consultants spend much of their time networking or building a clientele through established clients or making "cold" calls to people they don't know personally. Consultants' duties are divided between geoscience activities and the business and management side of running a company. Consultants must keep abreast of the latest news relating to the industry in which they work. Reading industry magazines and journals and browsing Internet sites are a daily activity. Not only does the consultant learn about what's happening in the industry from these sources, but industry sources also provide inspiration for obtaining new clients.

Training and Education

Consulting usually comes after years of experience working as a geologist for a major company or a large, aggressive independent firm. These organizations provide much of the education and training you'll need to become successful in the field in general. Once you've proven yourself in the industry, then you can set out to work as an independent consultant. In this field, being a generalist is an advantage, so be careful not to allow yourself to be pigeonholed into a specific niche, such as focusing solely on one basin or land formation. Years of experience and a broad scope of knowledge of all types of reservoirs, plus the ability to apply what you learn in one area to other areas, will help you succeed as a consultant.

Possible Employers

Engineering consulting firms, government agencies, oil field services, and equipment suppliers employ petroleum and mining geology consultants. Because of the cyclical nature of the oil and gas and mineral and mining industries, hiring on a contractual basis is common. This allows companies the freedom to discontinue the services of a worker without having the burden of paying benefits and severance packages. In particular, new companies and smaller firms seek consultant's services because their futures are less stable. Large, established companies expanding into a new territory may also procure the services of a consultant knowledgeable in a particular area. Local, state, and federal governments are top employers of consultants, whose independent and expert opinion may be solicited to evaluate the geological safety of structures such as dams and bridges.

Career Outlook

The career outlook for industry consultants is expected to be about the same as for traditionally employed workers in the petroleum industry—which is to say favorable. A greater number of jobs will be available as a mining consultant than as a full-time mining geologist, due mainly to the greater expense of starting up mining excavations and the lower return on the investment. The exception is overseas consulting work; in this case, there are abundant opportunities for consultants of all kinds. For those seeking a bit of adventure, overseas consulting could be an excellent choice.

Salary and Compensation

Although it is more risky than working for a large company, working as a consultant can be a lucrative career choice. This is mainly because consultants tend to have extensive experience and training and education. With more discoveries will come more royalties and six-figure salaries are not uncommon. Keep in mind, however, that you'll have to pay for your own healthcare and any time off is unpaid vacation or sick time.

Additional Job Titles

This chapter discussed geology jobs in the oil and mining industries in general terms, yet there are additional, more specialized jobs for geologists available in smaller numbers in these fields. This section describes, in brief, other careers or job titles worth exploring through further online research.

Economic geology integrates the science of geology and the practical discipline of mining within the constraints of economics. These geologists study mineral deposits, explore for new resources, participate in the development and mining of ore deposits, and help dispose of waste materials from mining activities in economically feasible ways; Cutting costs and turning a profit are of major concern to these geologists; consequently, economic geologists are very appealing to companies and organizations.

Exploration geologists in both the petroleum industry and the mining field seek out new oil and mineral reserves. Exploration for new resources involves developing and using geophysical detection methods similar to those discussed previously in this chapter. This is a more specialized type of geologist, working only in this area.

Production geologists work with known reserves. Some of the work of these geologists has been described already. Some of these geologists' duties include underground sampling and mapping, geological interpretation, monitoring and planning definition drilling, assisting in drive layouts, and reserve calculations.

Mineralogists analyze and classify minerals and precious stones according to composition and structure. Since minerals are defined as naturally occurring solid substances, there is a tremendous range of ideas and processes that can be studied, including everything from the soil surface to the center of the earth to the mineral content of other planets.

Stratigraphers help locate minerals by studying the distribution and arrangement of sedimentary rock layers and by examining the fossil and mineral content of these layers. They are interested in relative dating, aiming to determine, for example, if a sandstone formation originated as a beach or as the fill in a river or stream channel. From an analysis of a rock bed or core sample, these geologists can diagnose what the environment was like when the rock formed, including whether there might be a rich source of oil or minerals nearby.

7

Path 2: Environmental Geology

Although most geology graduates enter the petroleum and mining industries (about 60 percent and 20 percent, respectively), more and more geologists are choosing to put their expertise to work in the environmental sector. Our society has become increasingly aware of the need to maintain the Earth's natural environmental systems, restore damaged environments, and at the same time meet our legitimate and growing need for more materials and energy. And it's geologists who can perform these tasks.

Geologists play an important part in studying, protecting, and reclaiming the environment. Some geologists design and monitor waste disposal sites and help locate safe sites for hazardous waste facilities and landfills. Others help clean up contaminated land and water resources, try to preserve water supplies, and help private companies and governments comply with numerous and complex environmental regulations. Still others work in risk assessment to predict natural hazards, such as earthquakes, volcanic eruptions, floods, and tidal waves.

There are two main paths that environmental earth science professionals with a focus on geology can take. The first consists of scientists with strong backgrounds in mathematics, earth physics, and geochemistry. Consultants and specialist companies employ these geologists to provide expertise on water migration and waste management disposal from the municipal to the national level. The second includes traditional earth scientists involved in biological and sociological applications. These geologists combine degrees in several areas, such as geology, physics, or engineering. They find employment in companies dealing with environmental problems, such as drainage of wetlands or building on flood lands.

The scope of environmental geology is vast and it would be impossible to cover the breadth of work environmental geologists do in only one chapter. In fact, whole books are dedicated to this important work. This chapter describes in broad strokes the types of activities undertaken by those working in this important aspect of geology. This chapter also describes the work of hydrogeologists, another subset of geology. We've included it in this chapter because much of the work of hydrogeologists corresponds with that of environmental geologists in general.

Environmental Geologists

Environmental geologists conduct research to identify, reduce, and eliminate sources of pollutants or hazards that affect people and wildlife and their environments. Environmental geologists analyze and report measurements or observations of air, food, water, soil, and other sources and recommend ways to clean and preserve the environment. Understanding the issues involved in protecting the environment—degradation, conservation, recycling, and replenishment—is central to the work of environmental geologists, who often use their skills and knowledge to design and monitor waste disposal sites, preserve water supplies, and reclaim contaminated land and water to comply with federal environmental regulations. Environmental geologists study and work with earth materials and processes; soils and how they shape the environment; natural hazards, including landslides, earthquakes, and flooding; volcanic activity; water processing, supply, and use; water pollution and treatment; waste management; energy production; global environmental change; air pollution; and landscape development.

Environmental geologists spend part of their time in the field at specific sites gathering data and part of their time in their offices analyzing the data they've collected. In the field, they perform and supervise sampling work, well installation, and other related tasks, especially during the warmer months of the year. Other aspects of fieldwork include collecting water, air, and soil samples from a variety of terrains. In the office, they write reports, summarize and analyze lab data, generate sampling plans, and compute costs for project work.

Environmental geologists often work as site investigators. If there is to be new construction on a proposed site, an environmental geologist may be hired to examine the site for potential environmental problems; investigate local, state, and federal records for the site and all surrounding sites; and check historical use of the property and all surrounding properties. Geologists visiting a site will be inspecting it for potential environmental problems, such as underground tanks, improperly stored chemicals, lead, asbestos, and a multitude of other potential hazards. If soil or groundwater contamination is actually found at a particular site, environmental geologists will determine how extensive the contamination is and develop and implement a remediation plan. Many methods can be used to accomplish this, such as tank testing, soil sampling, and sampling of suspect substances.

Environmental geologists may also work as consultants. Generally speaking, an environmental consulting firm and the geologists employed by one work with businesses to assist them in complying with federal, state, and local environmental regulations. Businesses in need of an environmental consultant are typically operations that could potentially impact air, soil, and groundwater quality. It is the consultant's job to become completely familiar with the business's methods of operation and make recommendations to improve its overall compliance with regulations. For example, the National Environmental Policy Act (NEPA; epa.gov/compliance/nepa/) requires businesses to prepare environmental impact statements or assessments for proposed facilities that could have a deleterious effect on the environment. The Resource Conservation and Recovery Act (RCRA; search under access. gpo.gov) governs the creation and disposal of hazardous waste. The Clean Air Act (search under epa.gov) provides requirements for cleaner burning power plants and automobiles, control of fugitive emissions of hazardous air pollutants, fuel efficiency, and other conditions. To a somewhat lesser extent, depending upon what materials the business is working with, geologists may rely on the guidelines of the Clean Water Act and the Atomic Energy Act, both of which can also be found by searching the epa.gov website.

Environmental geologists, having accumulated a certain measure of experience and expertise in a field, may serve as experts in providing testimony for various types of legal cases. These experts investigate the site or situation and provide technical support and reports on hazardous conditions and contaminant transport just to name a few. They oversee the work of those who assess sites for contamination problems during a potential real estate transaction. So, they may also conduct forensic investigations on contaminated water supplies involving *Escherichia coli* and metals and on the activities of consultants conducting environmental investigations for real-estate transactions.

Training and Education

While a bachelor's degree is adequate for a few entry-level positions, across all subcategories of geology, there is an increasing demand for geologists with a graduate degree, especially a master's degree. After obtaining a four-year degree in geology, many students proceed to a master's degree with a specialization in environmental geology or a subfield, such as hydrogeology. A master's degree is the minimum educational requirement for most entry-level applied research positions in private industry, in state and federal agencies, and at state geological surveys. Only a small percentage of students progress to a doctoral degree in environmental geoscience; most of those pursuing doctoral degrees intend to enter teaching at the college or university level.

Undergraduate environmental geology majors should focus on data analysis and physical geography, particularly if they are interested in studying pollution abatement, water resources, or ecosystem protection, restoration, or management. Understanding the geochemistry of inorganic compounds is becoming increasingly important in developing remediation goals. Those students interested in working in the environmental or regulatory fields, either in environmental consulting firms or for federal or state governments, should take courses in hydrology, hazardous-waste management, environmental legislation, chemistry, fluid mechanics, and geologic logging. An understanding of environmental regulations and government permit issues also is valuable for those planning to work with mining and oil and gas extraction companies.

The skills a graduate is expected to acquire include environmental site assessment and ground investigation—the ability to investigate a site where a potential problem exists. This includes the acquisition, management, and analysis of the information, along with the knowledge of technological methods. In addition, graduates must have an awareness of possible preventive and remedial measures.

The following is a list of courses an environmental geology student might take:

Geochemistry of the Earth's surface
Environmental geochemistry
Engineering geology
Hydrogeology
Groundwater geophysics
Groundwater modeling
Quaternary stratigraphy
Geophysical field methods
Water resource geochemistry
Environmental resource planning
Land use planning
Toxicology for industry
Monitoring and evaluating work environments
Natural resources policy

In addition to typical coursework, there are several other areas in which environmental geologists should focus. First, computer training in spreadsheets, databases, management, programming, and field instrumentation, as well as specific programs used in environmental geology, are a must in order to be attractive candidates for employers. Fieldwork experience is also essential; you can gain it through coursework as well as internships and summer jobs. Finally, environmental geologists must have strong writing skills in order to write reports and other documents; take classes outside of your major in order to hone these skills.

Possible Employers

Local, state, and federal governments are employers of substantial numbers of geologists. One federal example is the U.S. Geological Survey (USGS; usgs.gov), a division of the U.S. Department of the Interior. The USGS provides the nation with information to describe and understand the Earth. The information is used to minimize loss of life and property from natural disasters; manage water, biological, energy, and mineral resources; enhance and protect quality of life; and contribute to wise economic and physical development. The USGS maintains several information and data centers that provide information on earthquakes, landslides, water resources, and more.

Those working for the government are generally involved in monitoring and regulating industries, companies, and municipal governments and the effects these institutions have on the environment. For example, an environmental geologist working for a federal government agency might evaluate wastewater treatment facilities that dispose of their effluent in oceans. They would issue permits on behalf of the government for the safe disposal of waste and citations to those to violate rules and regulations. Those working for the government to determine policy may help identify how human behavior can be modified in the future to avoid such problems as groundwater contamination and depletion of the ozone layer.

Some environmental geologists work in research and development for many different kinds of employers. For example, an environmental geologists might work for a company that is developing and producing alternative landfill cover designs, testing them for temperature, infiltration, soil moisture, and flow rates to see which is the most efficient and effective. Or one might work for a technology company developing computing and simulation tools for use by the environmental industry for research and application.

Environmental geologists may be part of the training and development team for a company that frequently encounters environmental issues. Training often focuses on educating employees about governmental rules and regulations as they apply to the work the company does or a product it produces. For example, a geologist may develop a training module on the Clean Air Act or a course about hazardous materials for a mining and manufacturing company.

Many environmental geologists work at consulting firms, advising and helping businesses and government agencies comply with environmental policy. They are generally hired to solve problems. When entering the field, environmental geologists thinking of working for consulting firms should consider the type of firm and the scope of the projects it undertakes. In larger firms, environmental geologists are more likely to engage in large, long-term projects in which their role will mesh with those of workers in other scientific disciplines. In smaller specialty firms, however, they may be responsible for many skills beyond traditional environmental disciplines, such as working with environmental laws and regulations, making environmental risk assessments, writing technical proposals, giving presentations to managers and regulators, and working with other specialists on a variety of issues, including engineering remediation. Some environmental geologists work in managerial positions, usually after spending some time performing research or learning about environmental laws and regulations.

Career Outlook

The field of environmental geology is one of the areas of highest demand within the geosciences. The United States produces billions of tons of solid, liquid, and gaseous waste every year. To deal with the threat these wastes pose to the environment, federal and state governments have created complex guidelines for the shipment, storage, disposal, and cleanup of these products, resulting in the need for environmental geologists to help organizations comply with these rules. There is also a growing need for earth scientists to apply their knowledge to help developing countries manage their waste and the by-products of increasing industrialization. Further job opportunities will be spurred by a continued general awareness regarding the need to monitor the quality of the environment, to interpret the impact of human actions on terrestrial and aquatic ecosystems, and to develop strategies for restoring ecosystems. Additionally, a fairly recent shift in focus from reactive solutions to preventive management will provide many new opportunities for environmental geologists in consulting roles. More and more talent will be required to help minimize damage to the environment, and innovative people will always be required by the environmental protection industry. Today's environmental geology graduates should expect little difficulty in finding employment opportunities.

Salary and Compensation

According to the U.S. Department of Labor, environmental geologists average about $51,080 in annual earnings. The majority of those working earn between $39,100 and $67,360. The lowest 10 percent of workers earn less than $31,610, whereas the highest 10 percent earn more than $85,940. According to the National Association of Colleges and Employers, beginning salary offers in July 2005 for graduates with bachelor's degrees in an environmental science field in general averaged $31,366 a year.

Median annual earnings in the industries employing the largest number of environmental geologists are as follows:

Federal government	$73,530
Management, scientific, and technical consulting services	$51,190
Architectural, engineering, and related services	$49,160
Local government	$48,870
State government	$46,850

Hydrologists

Hydrology is the branch of geology that studies water and its quality, distribution, and conservation. Hydrologists work with groundwater, water deep under the earth's surface, and even atmospheric water. The term hydrogeology is often used interchangeably with hydrology although some make the distinction that hydrogeology deals specifically with the distribution and movement of groundwater in soil and rocks.

Hydrologists study the distribution, circulation, and physical properties of underground and surface waters. They study the form and intensity of precipitation, its rate of infiltration into the soil, its movement through the Earth, and its return to the ocean and atmosphere. The work they do is particularly important in environmental preservation and remediation in that they assist in minimizing the environmental impacts of pollution, waterborne diseases, erosion, and sedimentation, and they study the impact of public and industrial water supply, water quality, and wastewater on the wetland habitats of fish and wildlife.

Hydrology is important to a variety of fields outside of geology. For example, the flow of water and how it penetrates surface soil and matter is valuable to advancing the areas of soil science, agriculture, and civil engineering. The movement of deeper water formations helps with urban planning, environmental conservation, and in the petroleum and mining industries. Hydrologists' work is particularly vital to flood control and environmental preservation, including water decontamination. Hydrologists use their knowledge of the physical landscape and history of the Earth to protect the environment, study the properties of underground and surface waters, locate water and energy resources, predict natural disasters and geologic hazards, and offer environmental site assessments and advice on hazardous waste remediation.

Most hydrologists use sophisticated techniques and instruments as a general part of their work. These include remote sensing devices, programs for collecting and running data, and computer modeling to monitor the change in regional and global waters. Some hydrologists working with surface water use sensitive stream-measuring devices to assess flow rates and the quality of water.

Like many geologists, most entry-level hydrologists spend the majority of their time in the field, while more experienced workers devote much of their time to office or laboratory work. Many beginning hydrologists and some environmental scientists, such as environmental ecologists and environmental chemists, often take field trips that involve physical activity. Hydrologists in the field may work in warm or cold climates and in all kinds of weather. Indeed, travel to meet with prospective clients or investors is often a part of the job.

Training and Education

Students interested in the field of hydrology should take courses in the physical sciences, geophysics, chemistry, engineering science, soil science, mathematics, aquatic biology, atmospheric science, geology, oceanography, hydrogeology, and the management or conservation of water resources. In some cases, graduates with a bachelor's degree in a hydrologic science are qualified for positions in environmental consulting and planning regarding water quality or wastewater treatment, although these positions tend to go to those with graduate degrees. Curricula for advanced degrees often emphasize the natural sciences.

For hydrologists who enter the field of consulting, courses in business, finance, marketing, or economics may be useful. In addition, combining hydrology training with other disciplines such as engineering, or a technical degree coupled with a master's degree in business administration, qualifies students for the widest range of jobs. Because international work is becoming increasingly common, knowledge of a second language is also a valuable skill.

Computer skills are essential for prospective hydrologists. Students who have some experience with computer modeling, data analysis and integration, digital mapping, remote sensing, and geographic information systems will be the most prepared to enter the job market. As with other aspects of geology, knowledge of the Geographic Information System (GIS) and Global Positioning System (GPS) is vital.

Hydrologists must have excellent interpersonal skills because they usually work as part of a team with other scientists, engineers, and technicians. Strong oral and written communication skills also are essential in order to write technical reports and research proposals and communicate technical and research results to company managers, regulators, and the public. Those involved in fieldwork must have physical stamina to work in a variety of conditions.

The American Institute of Hydrology (AIH; aihydro.org) offers certification programs in professional hydrology. The AIH is the only national organization to offer certification to professionals in all fields of hydrology. Certification is recommended for those seeking advancement or those who wish to upgrade their knowledge.

The AIH also offers the Fulbright Scholar Program, which features nine awards in geology, including awards in water resources or water engineering in Brazil, Canada, India, Israel, the Philippines, and the United Arab Emirates. Awards for both faculty and professionals range from two months to an academic year. While many awards specify project and host institution, there are a number of open "All Disciplines" awards that allow candidates to propose their own project and determine their host institution affiliation. Foreign language skills are needed in some countries, but most Fulbright lecturing assignments are in English.

Possible Employers

The federal government and colleges and universities are large employers of hydrologists in research positions. Due to the increase of recreational boating and other water sports, which has led to a range of environmental concerns, government agencies and private organizations hire hydrologists to analyze and suggest ways to relieve the pressure on public waterways. Hydrologists working for the government in the environmental sector may spend much of their time testing water in order to solve water quality problems at residential and industrial sites. In general, hydrologists working for the government or in academia may need to design programs and write grant proposals in order to continue their data collection and research.

Many other hydrologists work for consulting firms that focus on a particular kind of environmental problem or concern. These firms will hire geologists with experience in a certain area. For example, a firm may focus on water and wastewater infrastructure (water filtration plants) and solid waste or landfill design. Companies may also be contracted to clean up underground storage tank leaks and prepare environmental impact statements. The main duties of hydrologists working for these companies would be determining if environmental threats from toxic and radioactive substances are present in the ground or nearby water features. They would accomplish this by collecting water and subsurface soil samples, which are then sent to labs for chemical analysis, and install and collect samples from groundwater monitoring wells to determine if pollutants have contaminated the drinking water supply. They examine the types and concentrations of pollutants in the groundwater, and the distance they would have to travel to get into the nearest drinking water supply. The ultimate goal is to monitor, and if necessary, clean up contaminants in soil and groundwater that could have a significant impact on human health or the environment.

Career Outlook

Similar to environmental geology, hydrogeology is a segment of geology that is in great demand. An increasing world population and the quest for an improved environment will see substantial demands for these groundwater geologists.

In total, hydrologists hold about 8,000 jobs in the United States. Many more people with a focus in hydrology hold environmental science faculty positions in colleges and universities (see Chapter 10 for more information on working in academia). Of these 8,000 jobs, 22 percent of these hydrologists are employed in architectural, engineering, and related services, and 18 percent work for management, scientific, and technical consulting services. In 2004, the federal government employed about 2,500 hydrologists, mostly within the U.S. Department of the Interior for the USGS and within the U.S. Department of Defense. Another 15 percent worked for state agencies, such as state geological surveys and state departments of conservation. About 5 percent of hydrologists were self-employed, most as consultants to industry or government.

Job growth for hydrologists is strongest with private consulting firms, although opportunities in general are increasing as the U.S. population grows and moves to more environmentally sensitive locations. For example, as people migrate toward coastal regions, hydrologists will be needed to assess building sites for potential geologic hazards and to mitigate the effects of natural hazards such as floods and landslides. Hydrologists also will be needed to conduct research on hazardous-waste sites in order to determine the impact of hazardous pollutants on soil and ground water so that engineers can design remediation systems. Demand is growing for hydrologists who understand both the scientific and engineering aspects of waste remediation.

Federal and state geological surveys depend to a large extent on the public climate or interest in environmental issues and the current budget. Thus, job security for hydrologists within a state survey may be cyclical. During periods of economic recession, layoffs may occur in consulting firms. The good news is that layoffs are much less likely for those working for the government.

Salary and Compensation

Earnings for hydrologists are comparable to other environmental science workers. According to the U.S. Department of Labor, hydrologists annually earn about $61,510. The majority of persons earn between $47,080 and $77,910, with the lowest 10 percent earning less than $38,580, and the highest 10 percent earning more than $94,460. In 2005, the average salary for hydrologists in managerial, supervisory, and nonsupervisory positions was $77,182.

Additional Job Titles

Petrologists study rocks in general, including their occurrence, structural origins (petrogenesis), mineral content, and texture. Among other types of analysis, petrologists study extremely thin sections of rocks with special microscopes in order to learn more about the conditions that formed the rocks and minerals. This gives scientists a better idea of what the environment was like in that part of the planet where the rocks originated.

Geomorphologists study landforms and the Earth's surface sediments. They examine how elements such as air, water, and ice, shape the landscape. Geomorphologists map landforms shaped by erosion or deposition. They are also "landscape-detectives" working out the history of a landscape, such as those formed by receding glaciers. They ask questions about how the Rocky Mountains or Grand Canyon were formed. Astrogeomorphologists are similar to geomorphologists except that they study lunar and planetary surfaces.

Oceanographers and marine geologists study and map the ocean floor, collecting information using remote sensing devices aboard ships or on underwater research craft. More specifically, marine geologists compile data about the shape of the ocean floors (topography), the distribution and type of bottom sediments, the composition and structure of the underlying rocks, and the geologic processes that have been at work throughout the seafloor's history. Using this information, they assess the mineral resources of the seafloor and predict the location of hazards, among other things.

Sedimentologists are those working in sedimentology, a branch of geology that is concerned with understanding the characteristics of sediments and the processes that form them. Sedimentary rocks cover most of the Earth's surface and serve as a historical record of weather events. Sedimentologists apply their understanding of modern processes to historically formed sedimentary rocks, allowing them to understand how they formed.

Structural geologists study the destruction of and the wear and tear on rocks by looking at rock composition and structure. Structural geology is the branch of geology that deals with the processes that transform and shape rocks into another shape, arrangement, or even material. This is important to many aspects of geology, in particular to petroleum and mining geology, because folded and compressed rock forms traps for the accumulation of fluids such as petroleum and natural gas. Deposits of gold, silver, copper, lead, zinc, and other metals, are also commonly located in structurally complex areas. Finally, structural geology is a critical part of engineering geology, in which defects such as faults may affect the stability of dams, roads, and mines.

Volcanologists study the chemical and physical evolution of rocks and minerals, particularly volcanoes, lava, and magma. Volcanology is a hazardous field because sudden and unexpected eruptions may occur while scientists are on the site collecting rock and lava samples. One major focus of the field is how to accurately predict volcanic eruptions, something volcanologists have been working on for many years.

8

Path 3: Quantitative Geology

The title of this chapter may be confusing to some. That's because there is no formal category of "quantitative geology," yet the meaning of the phrase is specific to a certain type of potential career path for those pursuing geology undergraduate degrees. Quantitative refers to that which is measurable; it is a method of studying the properties of something using numbers and hard data. Quantitative analysis involves measuring variables and conducting chemical analyses. Quantitative study spans the spectrum of topics that can be researched and analyzed, from the hard to the soft sciences. In particular, quantitative geology means attributing a numerical value to the physical properties of rocks.

In this chapter, you'll learn about various geologically based career paths in which a head for numbers will come in handy. These jobs are for those who believe that everything can be measured and quantified. If you've always fancied yourself a bit of a math wiz, then the career paths featured in this chapter may be appealing to you.

Geophysicists

In general, physicists explore and identify basic principles and laws governing motion and gravitation, the macroscopic and microscopic behavior of gases, the structure and behavior of matter, the generation of and transfer between energy, and the interaction of matter and energy. In particular, geophysics applies these physical theories and measurements to discover various properties relating to the Earth. Geophysics includes the branches of seismology (earthquakes and elastic waves); geothermometry (heating of the

Earth, the flow of heat, volcanology, and hot springs); hydrology (ground and surface water); atmospheric electricity and Earth magnetism; and geochronology (dating of Earth history). The science of geophysics is typically used to search for mineral and petroleum deposits; however, it can also be used to identify environmental hazards, evaluate sites for potential new construction of buildings, and create images of planetary surfaces. Applying geophysics to locate deposits of oil, gas, minerals, and water is called exploration geophysics. Solid earth geophysics is the study of plate tectonics or the interior structure of the Earth.

Originally, this field of study developed in order to study and predict earthquakes, an ongoing area of research. A burst of scientific activity occurred in the 1500s when gravity was explained and again in the 1700s with observations of the Earth's magnetism. In the early 1900s, advances in the creation and use of various instruments generated rapid progress in geophysics, which led to the theory of plate tectonics in the 1960s. The latest innovations in the field are a result of high-tech and computerized instrumentation, including the three-dimensional seismic method (to be discussed later in the chapter). In particular, during the last several decades, geophysicists have created and commercialized numerous technical innovations, changing the process of natural resource exploration and production.

Geophysicists study the Earth in order to build houses, schools, and hospitals in safe locations; find and develop oil, mineral, and gas deposits; increase our supplies of fresh groundwater; and advance this area of scientific inquiry. Instruments to sense and measure sound, electricity, magnetism, gravity, radio waves, and radar are the tools of the trade for these workers. With these tools, geophysicists identify the properties of rock and soil; search for groundwater, oil, gas, and minerals; map earthquake faults; assess strong ground motion characteristics (the movement of the Earth's tectonic plates); and delineate buried hazardous waste. Most geophysicists work in offices and labs conducting laboratory work and research, although fieldwork may also be a part of the job. When fieldwork is required, it is often, although not always, conducted in remote areas. Finally, good writing skills are required to prepare environmental site assessments and reports and research studies for publication.

Geophysicists design and perform a variety of meticulous experiments using a wide range of equipment, including lasers, particle accelerators, telescopes, mass spectrometers, magnetometers, various electromagnetic sensors, and radioactivity detectors. Seismic technology is the most common and wide-ranging technology in use in geophysics today. The principle is similar to sonar technology in that seismic or shock waves penetrate the surface of the Earth and return distortions that give scientists some idea of what may exist below ground. Geophysicists are increasingly using satellite data for use in their own interpretations. These data are used to identify surface conditions before conducting surveys and mapping the Earth, its resources, and environmental conditions. Many minerals, oil deposits, and natural features are found because they have unique geophysical characteristics that are only identifiable by such a range of highly sensitive instruments.

Petroleum Geophysicists

Geophysicists working in the petroleum industry have three main career paths they can pursue: acquisition, processing, or interpretation of seismic data. Acquisition geophysicists spend most of their time in the field with a crew collecting seismic data. They are in charge of the information collection from the beginning of the design phase, and they decide what instruments to use and how to collect the data. After the information is gathered, the reflected seismic waves are recorded in the field and transformed into digital recordings, which are written on computer disk in binary form by the processing geophysicist. The processing geophysicist manipulates and analyzes the information and creates images that can be viewed. They revise and test the information using complicated computer programs to better understand the data. They then consult with interpretation geophysicists to ensure that all available geological information is taken into account. Interpretation geophysicists are involved in every aspect of the seismic work from planning the survey, overseeing the data collection, interacting with the processors, and finalizing the interpretation. Interpretation geophysicists interpret the data to further scientific research in the field. This information can then be applied to many different fields.

Environmental Geophysicists

Environmental geophysics is a relatively new field, in which the primary objective is to identify, map, or predict the presence and movement of surface water and groundwater and contaminants. Their goal is to identify situations in which environments have been contaminated or are at risk of contamination and suggest means of preventing further contamination. Most environmental geophysicists spend roughly equal amounts of time in the field collecting data and in the office analyzing data; work can be in either rural or urban environments.

Training and Education

A variety of skills and talents are required to be successful in this field. The most valuable traits a geophysicist possesses are an analytical mind, an affinity for technical or engineering work, and excellent organizational skills. In addition, the ability to apply physics and higher math to solving practical problems will be a great benefit in your career. Finally, you should be able to work well both in a team and on your own.

Those interested in working as a geophysicist should have an undergraduate double major or a major and minor in geology and physics. Strong coursework in both areas will make you a more appealing candidate to potential employers. Typical physics courses include electromagnetism, optics, thermodynamics, atomic physics, and quantum mechanics. Graduate students usually concentrate on a subfield of geophysics, such as seismology or condensed matter, although many begin studying for their doctorate immediately after receiving their bachelor's degree.

The minimum education for those wishing to work as a geophysicist is a bachelor's degree in either geophysics, physics, math, or geology. A double major in any of these areas will make you a more marketable candidate, as will significant coursework in computer science or software applications. Experience in making geophysical observations in the field or the lab, analyzing numerical data, and honing general technological skills will be beneficial. Persons with only a bachelor's degree in physics or astronomy are not qualified to enter most research jobs, but you may qualify for a wide range of positions related to engineering, mathematics, computer science, environmental science, and, for those with the appropriate background, some non-science fields, such as finance. Those who meet state certification requirements can become high school physics teachers, an occupation in great demand in many school districts; however, most states require new teachers to obtain a master's degree in education within a certain time.

Obtaining a master's degree or Ph.D. in geophysics will give you greater access to the best jobs. The following are a sample of courses you might take while pursuing further study in geophysics:

Computing and numerical methods
Sedimentology
Stratigraphic principles and maps
Vibrations and waves
Electromagnetism
Tectonophysics
Statistics
Deformation processes
Sedimentary processes
Igneous and metamorphic petrology
Field skills
Atmosphere and ocean dynamics

Physics and relativity
Global seismology
Hydrocarbon and mineral resources
Volcanic processes
Hydrogeology and groundwater contamination
Basin dynamics and petroleum systems
Plate tectonics and geodynamics
Dynamics of particles and rigid bodies

Having a Ph.D. is necessary for the majority of jobs in the field of geology Many people begin their careers in a postdoctoral research position, in which they may work with experienced geophysicists as they learn about their specialty and develop ideas they will use in later work. While initial work is often conducted under the close supervision of senior scientists, after some experience, geophysicists perform increasingly complex tasks and work more independently. Those who develop new products or processes sometimes form their own companies or join new firms to exploit their own ideas. Experience, either in academic laboratories or through internships, fellowships, or work-study programs in industry, is always useful for advancing their career. Some employers of research physicists, particularly in the information technology industry, prefer to hire individuals with several years of postdoctoral experience.

The need for computer savvy and skills cannot be overstated in this area of study. Geophysicists frequently use specialized computer skills in their day-to-day work and many are actively involved in the development of hardware and software that will further assist their study. These efforts have produced highly sophisticated equipment and computer applications capable of creating complex graphics and images. Computer technology has become an integral component in geophysics, especially for processing huge, offshore seismic surveys.

Possible Employers
Geophysicists may work independently or as a member of a team with other professionals in public or private sectors, industry, commerce, scientific research, or health and education fields. Companies involved in field acquisition and data processing related to natural resource exploration employ large numbers of geophysicists. Other employers include engineering companies, environmental monitoring corporations or institutions, archeological digs, research institutes, universities and colleges, data management firms, the government and NASA, mining companies, consulting engineering firms, mapping service companies, and instrument manufacturing and development firms.

A large number of geophysicists work in research and development, in both basic and applied research. Basic research is that which advances thought in the field, while applied research builds upon the discoveries made through basic research to develop new instruments, products, and processes. Much of the geophysics research conducted today is done in small- or medium-sized laboratories, although experiments in plasma, nuclear, and high-energy physics, as well as other specialized areas, require extremely large, expensive equipment, such as particle accelerators. While geophysics research may require extensive experimentation in laboratories, these scientists still spend time in offices planning, recording, analyzing, and reporting on their laboratory work.

The largest number of geophysicists finds employment in the petroleum industry. Employers of petroleum geophysicists include:

Oil and gas companies
Seismic data processing firms
Well-logging companies
Computer companies
Research firms
Colleges and universities
Government and environmental agencies
Geophysical equipment companies

Finally, a small number of physicists work in inspection, testing, quality control, and other production-related jobs in industry.

Career Outlook

There are only about 16,000 physicists working in the United States today and, of these, those concentrating on geophysics are only a small portion. Nearly 33 percent of physicists work for scientific research and development services firms, as well as for the government, colleges and universities, and private firms. Thus, many of the statistics available for the future outlook of this type of job focus on research and development.

According to government statistics, the overall employment of physicists is expected to grow more slowly than the average for all occupations through 2014. Federal research expenditures are the major source of physics-related research funds, especially for basic research and, although these funds are expected to increase at least until 2014, resulting in some growth in employment and opportunities, the limited science research funds available will result in competition for basic research jobs among Ph.D. holders. In addition, the need to cut programs in order to fund other areas, such as defense, may result in cuts to physics-related research programs. The need to replace physicists who retire or otherwise leave the occupation permanently will account for most expected job openings.

Although research and development expenditures in private industry will continue to grow, many research laboratories are expected to reduce their basic research programs, which include much physics research, in favor of applied or manufacturing research and product and software development. Nevertheless, persons with a background in physics continue to be in demand in the areas of information technology, semiconductor technology, and other applied sciences.

Recent increases in undergraduate physics enrollment may lead to growth in enrollment in graduate physics programs, resulting in an increase in the number of doctoral degrees granted, which will then intensify the competition for job openings. Opportunities may be more numerous for those with master's degrees, particularly graduates from programs preparing students for applied research and development, product design, and manufacturing positions in private industry. Many of these positions, however, will have titles other than physicist, such as engineer or computer scientist. In order to make yourself the most marketable candidate, be sure to have an area of focus or expertise, plenty of high-tech experience, and a substantial amount of experience in applied research. Despite competition for traditional physics research jobs, graduates with a physics degree at any level will find their knowledge of science and mathematics useful for entry into many other occupations.

Salary and Compensation

Those working in the field of physics tend to command an attractive salary. According to the U.S. Department of Labor, the median annual earnings of physicists are about $87,500. The middle 50 percent of those currently working in the field earn between $66,600 and $109,400, while the lowest 10 percent earn less than $49,450 and the highest 10 percent earned more than $132,800. In addition, the American Institute of Physics reported slightly higher earning for a survey conducted of their members, with a median annual salary of $104,000 in 2004 for members with Ph.D.s. Those with master's degrees commanded a median annual income of about $94,000, and those with bachelor's degrees earned a substantial $72,000. According to a 2005 National Association of Colleges and Employers survey, the average annual starting salary offer to physics doctoral degree candidates hoping to teach was $56,100. Finally, the federal government offers attractive wages. The average annual salary for physicists employed by the federal government is about $105,000, although this may be a result of the need for the government to employ highly trained and experienced scientists.

Geostatisticians

Statistics is the scientific application of mathematical principles to the collection, analysis, and presentation of numerical data. Statisticians contribute to scientific inquiry by applying their mathematical and statistical knowledge to the design of surveys and experiments; the collection, processing, and analysis of data; and the interpretation of the results. They also apply this knowledge to a variety of subject areas, such as biology, economics, engineering, medicine, public health, psychology, marketing, education, and even sports! Geostatisticians are those who deal with the statistics of geology.

Geostatistics concerns the use of geological data to evaluate the complexities of various models and the probabilities of things, such as finding hydrocarbons. Geostatisticians are scientists who apply statistical methods to geological information to determine factors such as grade and mineral concentration in different volumes of rock mass. These scientists tend to work in areas such as resource estimation and reporting of resources and reserves, but they are also involved with planning sampling programs.

One technique that is especially useful to geostatisticians is sampling—obtaining information about a type of rock or geological setting by surveying a small portion of the total. For example, to determine the composition of a mountain, geostatisticians may gather samples of rock from various points around or on the mountain—they certainly couldn't cover every square inch! Geostatisticians decide where and how to gather the data, determine the type and size of the sample group, and develop the survey. They also prepare instructions for workers who will collect and tabulate the data. Finally, they will analyze, interpret, and summarize the data using computer software.

In business and industry, geostatisticians play an important role in quality control and in product development and improvement. In a company that manufactures tools for use in the field, for example, geostatisticians might design experiments to determine the failure time of these tools when exposed to extreme weather conditions and frequent use on hard rock by putting them through tests until they break or wear down. Similarly, at a computer software firm, geostatisticians might help construct new statistical software packages to analyze data more accurately and efficiently. In addition to product development and testing, some geostatisticians also are involved in deciding what products a company should manufacture, how much to charge for them, and to whom the products should be marketed. They may also manage assets and liabilities, determining the risks and returns of certain investments.

Training and Education

Approximately 230 universities offer degree programs in statistics, biostatistics, or mathematics. Many other schools also offered graduate-level courses in applied statistics for students majoring in geology. Acceptance into graduate statistics programs does not require an undergraduate degree in statistics, although good training in mathematics is essential.

The recommended route for becoming a geostatistician is to gain a double major, or a major and a minor, in geology and statistics. Required statistical subjects include differential and integral calculus, statistical methods, mathematical modeling, and probability theory. Additional courses that undergraduates should take include linear algebra, design and analysis of experiments, applied multivariate analysis, and mathematical statistics.

Although employment opportunities exist for individuals with a bachelor's degree, in particular with the federal government, a master's degree in statistics or mathematics is usually the minimum educational requirement for most jobs. Research and academic positions in institutions of higher education, for example, require at least a master's degree, and usually a Ph.D., in statistics. Beginning positions in industrial research often require a master's degree combined with several years of experience.

Because computers are used extensively for statistical applications, a strong background in computer science is highly recommended. For positions involving quality and productivity improvement, training in engineering is also useful. Courses in economics and business administration are helpful for many jobs in market research, business analysis, and forecasting.

Good communication skills are important for prospective geostatisticians in industry, who often need to explain technical matters to persons without statistical expertise. An understanding of business and the economy also is valuable for those who plan to work in private industry.

Possible Employers

According to government statistics, statisticians in general hold about 19,000 jobs. Twenty percent of these jobs are with the federal government, where statisticians are concentrated in the Departments of Commerce, Agriculture, and Health and Human Services. Another 20 percent work for state and local governments, including state colleges and universities. Most of the remaining jobs are in private industry, especially in scientific research and development services, insurance carriers, and pharmaceutical and medical manufacturing.

In addition, many professionals with a background in statistics are among the 53,000 postsecondary mathematical science teachers.

Career Outlook

Career projections for statisticians in general and geostatisticians in particular are difficult to locate and interpret. That's because while employment of statisticians in general is projected to grow more slowly than average for all occupations throughout 2014, many jobs that require a degree in statistics do not carry the title "statistician." Despite the slow growth projection, opportunities should remain favorable for those with a degree in statistics.

The use of statistics is widespread and growing. Among graduates with a master's degree in statistics, those with a strong background in an allied field, such as geology, should have the best prospects of finding jobs related to their field of study. Federal agencies will hire statisticians in many fields, including demography, agriculture, consumer and producer surveys, and environmental quality. Because the federal government is one of the few employers that consider a bachelor's degree an adequate entry-level qualification, competition for entry-level positions with the government is expected to be strong for persons just meeting the minimum qualifications for statisticians.

Salary and Compensation

Statisticians command a range of salaries. According to the U.S. Department of Labor, the median annual earnings of statisticians are about $58,600. Of those working in all areas and holding a spectrum of degrees, the middle 50 percent earn between $42,800 and $80,900; the lowest 10 percent earn less than $32,900; and the highest 10 percent earn more than $100,500. The average annual salary for those working for the federal government in non-supervisory, supervisory, and managerial positions is about $81,300, while mathematical statisticians average $91,500. According to a 2005 survey by the National Association of Colleges and Employers, starting salary offers for graduates with a bachelor's degree in statistics only averaged $43,500 a year.

Astrogeologists

Astrogeology is the study of solid planetary bodies, including planets, moons, asteroids, and meteors. Astrogeology is sometimes considered a subfield of physics because astrogeologists use the principles of physics and mathematics to learn about the fundamental nature of the universe. They employ research techniques used to study the Earth's geology to understand the geology of astral bodies and how they are formed. For example, one may study the surface measurements of various planets, including Mars and the moon, in order to understand how these surfaces evolved over time. These scientists spend many hours literally staring into space using high-power telescopes.

In addition to researching how planets work, astrogeologists help plan and implement space missions designed to bring back geological artifacts. They are often interested in characterizing the current properties of the known planets and developing an understanding of the formation of planetary systems (core, mantle, crust, surface, hydrosphere, atmosphere, exosphere, rings, and satellites). They also study planetary processes (volcanism, tectonics, the impact of craters, and chemical evolution) in order to make predictions about the Earth's geological evolution. Astrogeologists study and analyze data acquired mainly from spacecraft and perform experimental laboratory analyses.

There are several fascinating research projects in this area. Galileo and Cassini are large, ongoing programs exploring the outer planets, although there are a variety of small spacecraft with focused objectives that will soon return new data gathered on asteroids, Mars, and comets. Researchers at the University of Arizona (UA; ua.edu) are studying Jupiter's volcanic moon, Io, and assembling a database containing all of Io's identified surface features and their latitude/longitude coordinates. Scientists at UA have made some startling discoveries, including that Io is home to more than 500 volcanoes and that, although it is about the size of the Earth's moon, Io has mountains on it that are higher than Mount Everest! Finally, scientists continue to study our own moon, attempting to make observations about its history through data collected by viewing the moon's surface in different wavelengths of light. The different wavelengths reveal variations in surface coloration and composition, which can be used to determine whether a given crater is older or younger than those around it, making it possible to reconstruct the history of the moon.

Training and Education

Astrogeologists tend to concentrate in three areas: astrology, geology, and physics. Students with a strong core of physics classes, in addition to astronomy research experience, are the most attractive to graduate school admissions committees. A bachelor of science (B.S.) degree in physics with extra astronomy and geology courses would provide more job opportunities than a B.S. in either astronomy or geology, should you decide to terminate your formal education with a bachelor's degree. Although it is hard to become an astrogeologist, most who get graduate degrees in the field are employed, one of the benefits of higher education.

Most astrogeology positions require a Ph.D. degree, which can take five or six years of graduate work. Admission to graduate schools generally requires completing an undergraduate geology/physics or astronomy/physics major with a B average or better and satisfactory performance on the Graduate Record Exam. Once admitted, the astronomy graduate students take advanced courses in astrogeology and astrophysics while beginning to undertake some research. The specific courses depend on the requirements of the department and on the student's research interests. After the first two years of course work, the graduate program generally requires research projects to be conducted under the supervision of faculty members, culminating in a Ph.D. dissertation. Recent university graduates start their careers at universities, colleges, and other institutions with postdoctoral research positions (one to three years of research work for people with new doctoral degrees) and research associateships that allow for full-time research. Many Ph.D. holders eventually teach at colleges and universities.

Master's degree holders usually do not qualify for basic research positions, but do qualify for many kinds of jobs requiring an astrogeologic or geophysics background, including positions in manufacturing and applied research and development. Increasingly, many master's degree programs are specifically preparing students for research and development that does not require a Ph.D. These programs teach students specific research skills that can be used in private industry. In addition, a master's degree coupled with state certification usually qualifies one for teaching jobs in high schools or at two-year colleges.

Those with bachelor's degrees are rarely qualified to fill positions in research or in teaching at the college level. They are, however, usually qualified to work as technicians or research assistants in engineering-related areas, in software development and other scientific fields, or in setting up computer networks and sophisticated laboratory equipment. Increasingly, some may qualify for applied research jobs in private industry or take on nontraditional roles, often in computer science, such as a systems analyst or database administrator. Some become science teachers in secondary schools. In addition, they are qualified to work in planetariums running science shows, to assist astronomers doing research, and to operate space-based and ground-based telescopes and other astronomical instrumentation.

College undergraduates planning careers in astrogeology must obtain a solid foundation in astronomy, physics, and mathematics. Specifically, a student planning to go on to graduate school should have had physics courses covering electricity and magnetism, atomic and nuclear physics, thermodynamics, statistical mechanics, and quantum theory.

Computer science, too, permeates all facets of astronomy today. In recent years, supercomputers have allowed astronomers to simulate processes that before were nearly impossible to study. A good grounding in computer science, therefore, will benefit you, especially if you're considering a specialty in theoretical astrogeology. In addition, a good scientist must also have the ability to read and write clearly and to communicate well with people, often across cultural boundaries. Do not neglect college courses in writing, the humanities, and the social sciences.

Possible Employers

Although astrogeologists are employed in all parts of the country, most work in areas in which universities, large research and development laboratories, or observatories are located. Most professional astrogeologists (about 55 percent) are either faculty members at universities and colleges, or affiliated with universities and colleges through observatories and laboratories. For these scientists, teaching is their major activity, although they may spend a portion of their time conducting research. Indeed, astrogeologists at leading colleges are a major source of research activity.

The majority of astrogeologists are directly employed by the federal government or by federally supported national observatories and laboratories. These employers tend to hire workers on the basis of research skills and experience. While the individual scientist may devote some time to research of personal interest, the employer most often defines the research topic. This is because governmental agencies such as the National Aeronautics and Space Administration (NASA; nasa.gov), the Naval Research Laboratory (NRL; nrl.navy.mil), and the U.S. Naval Observatory (usno. navy.mil) have very specific goals and interests.

About 10 percent of all astronomers work in business or private industry. Across various industries there are a large number of companies that hire those with astrogeological experience to conduct research. In practice, most companies protect their good employees, but the choice of work within a given company may be limited. In exchange for some loss of choice, there is the likelihood of getting a job that is technically challenging and that provides great opportunity for both intellectual and professional growth. Industrial employment offers a wide variety of nontechnical career paths as well. Although a Ph.D. is useful for industrial jobs, it is less often a requirement.

Astronomers working in planetariums, science museums, or in other public service positions provide an important information link between the world of professional astronomy and the general public. These jobs require a broad range of astronomy knowledge and the ability to communicate clearly and effectively with the public. Some jobs are available in secondary schools teaching physics or earth sciences, as well as in the science journalism field. Jobs in these categories generally do not require an advanced degree, although a Ph.D. or master's degree might prove useful at the more technical levels.

Career Outlook

Astrogeology is a fairly small field of study; because of this, there is keen competition for jobs in the field. Tenured teaching positions, in particular, are hard to come by, which is why many new Ph.D.s find themselves looking outside traditional areas for employment. In such a small and popular field, only those with a quality education, ability, and passion for the subject are likely to find a permanent position. Astronomy, physics, and geological training, however, emphasize a remarkably broad set of problem-solving skills. In fact, flexibility in terms of area of study and expertise will give you an advantage over others. With careful selection of graduate school courses and experiences, you can more easily transition into an interesting and productive career in a related field, such as industrial research, education, and public information.

Salary and Compensation

According to government statistics, the median annual earnings of astronomers in general are approximately $97,300. The middle 50 percent of these workers earn between $66,200 and $120,400, the lowest 10 percent earn less than $43,400, and the highest 10 percent earn more than $137,900. Scientists at national or government labs earn the highest median salary, followed by those employed by business or industry.

For those working at colleges and universities, the median salaries depend upon the size, quality, and competitiveness of the school. Starting salaries for assistant professors usually start at about $50,000 for nine to ten months (essentially a school year), while the range for senior professors is from $80,000 to $100,000 for nine to ten months of work. Many faculty members augment their salaries with summer work at their universities or with summer research support.

Additional Job Titles

Other quantitative jobs include those in the fields of geodesy, seismography, atmospheric geophysics, and geo- and paleomagnetics. Geodesists study the size and shape of the Earth, its gravitational field, tides, polar motion, and rotation. The measurements geodesists take are crucial to the study of climate change, the advance and retreat of ice sheets and glaciers, and the rise of the sea level.

Seismologists are mainly concerned with the study of the Earth's internal structure, its deep interior and dynamics, how the Earth was formed, and the physical phenomena that cause earthquakes. They interpret data from seismographs and other geophysical instruments to detect earthquakes and locate earthquake-related faults, and they draw upon the fundamentals of geology, material science, geodesy, and statistics in conducting their work. Seismology attracts considerable public interest and support because of its contributions to society in mitigating earthquake hazards, monitoring nuclear explosions, and finding oil.

Atmospheric geophysicists study the physics, chemistry, and dynamics of the atmosphere, particularly the two layers closest to Earth's surface, the stratosphere and troposphere. These layers are crucial to life because they regulate global temperature and provide protection from high-energy, atmospheric radiation. One of the most critical issues studies by these scientists today is global climate change. Much of their research is focused on monitoring fluctuations in the ozone layer, aerosols, levels of gases, and the effects of emissions from human activities such as aircraft, industry, and fossil fuel and biomass burning. The purpose of this research is to provide information in support of policies designed to respond to atmospheric changes that place great stress on our environment.

Geomagnetists and paleomagnetists study the geomagnetic field, from its core to space, to gain an understanding of Earth's structure, dynamics, and history. Specifically, geomagnetists measure the Earth's magnetic field and use measurements taken over the past few centuries to devise theoretical models to explain its origin, while paleomagnetists analyze fossil magnetization in rocks and sediments collected from the continents and oceans. Data collection from these scientists provides information on seafloor spreading, continental drift, and the movement of the Earth's polarity over time. Other key aspects of this type of study include the physics and chemistry of magnetic minerals or how minerals are formed and become magnetized, which is the area of specialization of rock magnetists. Results from all of these areas of scientific inquiry have been applied in recent years to understanding current environmental problems, as well as ancient climatic conditions.

9

Path 4: Careers in Museum Science

The goals of most geological museums are to conserve the geological heritage of the surrounding area through the collection, preparation, curation, conservation, and interpretation of mineral, rock, and fossil specimens. Most major geological museum collections include rocks, minerals, and fossils and their documentation as well as archival information in the form of maps, books, reprints, and photographs.

Geologists are employed in museums and libraries that collate and analyze data about the region's geological specimens. They act as researchers, curators, archivists, collections managers, and museum technicians and often play administrative roles as assistant or full directors. While some aspects of each position are similar, there are several differences in the nature of the work of these museum science professionals.

Archivists, Curators, and Conservators

Archivists and curators coordinate educational and public outreach programs, such as tours, workshops, lectures, and classes for museums and libraries. Although some duties of archivists and curators are similar, the types of items they deal with differ: Curators usually handle objects with cultural, biological, or historical significance, such as artifacts and specimens, while archivists handle mainly records and documents that are retained because of their importance and potential value in the future.

Curators administer the affairs of museums, nature centers, and historic sites. The head curator of the museum is usually called the museum director. Curators direct the acquisition, storage, and exhibition of collections, including negotiating and authorizing the purchase, sale, exchange, or loan of collections. They are also responsible for authenticating, evaluating, and categorizing the specimens in a collection. Curators oversee and help conduct the institution's research projects and related educational programs. Today, an increasing part of a curator's duties involves fundraising and promotion, which may include the writing and reviewing of grant proposals, journal articles, and publicity materials, as well as attendance at meetings, conventions, and civic events.

Conservators manage, care for, preserve, treat, and document artifacts and specimens—work that may require substantial historical, scientific, and archaeological research. They use x-rays, chemical testing, microscopes, special lights, and other laboratory equipment and techniques to examine objects and determine their condition, their need for treatment or restoration, and the appropriate method for preserving them. Conservators document their findings and treat items to minimize their deterioration or to restore them to their original state.

Finally, museum technicians assist curators by performing various preparatory and maintenance tasks on museum items. Some museum technicians also may assist curators with research. Archives' technicians help archivists organize, maintain, and provide access to historical materials. This is the entry-level job for someone hoping to advance to curator or archivist.

Training and Education

A Ph.D. is the usual requirement for museum work for geologists, but some entry-level positions, such as assistant curator, are open to geologists with a master's degree. Some archivists and curators work in archives or museums as technicians or assistants to gain experience while completing their formal education. Additionally, some museums offer summer field programs in paleontology and mineralogy for graduate or undergraduate college credit. These programs allow students to enter the field and gain hands-on, real-world experience under direct supervision of the professional staff of the museum. In general, employers look for those with a record of grants and peer-reviewed publications and strong leadership and management skills and experience.

Although archivists earn a variety of undergraduate degrees, including geology, most employers prefer a graduate degree in library science, with courses in archival science. A few institutions now offer master's degrees in archival studies, which is an increasingly attractive degree for many museums. Many colleges and universities offer courses or practical training in archival science as part of their geology, library science, or other curriculum. In addition, the Academy of Certified Archivists (certifiedarchivists.org) offers voluntary certification for archivists. The designation "Certified Archivist" is obtained by those with at least a master's degree and a year of appropriate archival experience. The certification process requires that candidates pass a written examination, and they must renew their certification periodically.

To work as a curator, most museums require at least a master's degree in either geology or archaeology or in museum studies. Many employers, however, prefer a doctoral degree, particularly for curators in natural history or science museums. Earning two graduate degrees—in museum studies (museology) and geology—will give you a distinct advantage in this competitive job market. That said, in small museums, you might be able to obtain a curatorial position even though you hold only a bachelor's degree. Because curators—particularly those in small museums—may have administrative and managerial responsibilities, courses in business administration, public relations, marketing, and fundraising also are recommended. Like archivists, curators need computer skills and experience with electronic databases. Many curators are also responsible for posting information on the Internet, so they need to be familiar with digital imaging, scanning technology, and copyright law.

When hiring conservators, employers look for a master's degree in conservation or in a closely related field, together with substantial experience. There are only a few graduate programs in museum conservation techniques in the United States, however, and competition to get into these programs is keen. In order to qualify for most of them, a student must have a background in chemistry, archaeology, geology, or similar, as well as work experience. For some programs, knowledge of a foreign language also is helpful. Conservation apprenticeships or internships as an undergraduate can enhance one's admission prospects. Graduate programs usually last from two to four years and the latter years typically include an internship. A few individuals enter conservation through apprenticeships with museums, nonprofit organizations, and conservators in private practice, so keep your eyes open to opportunities in these areas. Apprenticeship training, although accepted, is a more difficult route into the conservation profession than is formal training at a university.

Museum technicians usually need a bachelor's degree in an appropriate discipline of the museum's specialty, training in museum studies, or previous experience working in museums, particularly in the design of exhibits. Similarly, archives technicians usually need a bachelor's degree in library science, geology, or relevant work experience. Technician positions often serve as a stepping-stone for individuals interested in archival and curatorial work. Except in small museums, a master's degree is needed for advancement.

Relatively few schools grant a bachelor's degree in museum studies. More common are undergraduate minors or tracks of study that are part of an undergraduate degree in a related field, such as geology. Students would then pursue a graduate degree in museum studies. That said, many employers feel that, while museum studies are helpful, a thorough knowledge of the museum's specialty and museum work experience are more important.

As with most areas grounded in science, lifelong education is also necessary to remain relevant and in demand in this field. Continuing education, which enables archivists, curators, and museum technicians to keep up with developments in the field, is available through meetings, conferences, and workshops sponsored by archival, historical, and museum associations. In many cases, museums will even reimburse their employees to take courses and workshops and attend conferences.

Possible Employers

Archivists, curators, and museum technicians work for museums, governments, colleges and universities, corporations, and other institutions that require experts to preserve important records. In total, archivists, curators, and museum technicians hold about 27,000 jobs in the United States. About 34 percent of these workers are employed in museums, historical sites, and similar institutions, and 16 percent work for state and private educational institutions, mainly college and university libraries. Nearly 28 percent work for the federal, state, or local government. Most federal government curators work at the Smithsonian Institution (si.edu) and in archaeological and other museums and historic sites managed by the U.S. Department of the Interior (doi.gov). State and local governments also have numerous historical museums, parks, libraries, and zoos employing curators.

Many archives, including one-person shops, are very small and have limited opportunities for promotion. Archivists typically advance by transferring to a larger unit that has supervisory positions. Some large corporations that have archives or record centers employ archivists to manage the growing volume of records created or maintained as required by law or necessary to the firms' operations. Religious and fraternal organizations, professional associations, conservation organizations, major private collectors, and research firms also employ archivists and curators.

Career Outlook

Unfortunately, the competition for jobs as archivists, curators, and museum technicians is keen because qualified applicants outnumber job openings. For those wishing to work as an archivist, graduates with highly specialized training, such as master's degrees in both library science and geology, with extensive computer skills should have the best opportunities for jobs. A curator job is attractive to many people, and many applicants have the necessary training and knowledge of the subject, but there are only a few openings. Consequently, candidates may have to work part time, as an intern, or even as a volunteer assistant curator or research associate after completing their formal education. Substantial work experience in collection management, exhibit design, or restoration, as well as database management skills, will be necessary for permanent status. Specific geology experience and education will be most beneficial if you're looking for a job at a museum specializing in some aspect of geology.

The job outlook for conservators is generally more favorable, particularly for graduates of conservation programs. However, the competition is stiff for those applying to these programs, as there are a limited number of openings and applicants often need a technical background. Students who qualify and successfully complete the program, have knowledge of a foreign language, and are willing to relocate will have an advantage over less qualified candidates.

According to the U.S. Department of Labor, employment of archivists, curators, and museum technicians is expected to increase about as fast as the average for all occupations through 2014. That means that the number of jobs is expected to grow as public and private organizations emphasize establishing archives and organizing records and information and as public interest in science, history, and technology increases. While museum attendance has experienced a drop in recent years because of a weak economy, the long-term trend has been a rise in attendance, and this trend is expected to continue now that the economy is recovering. There is healthy public and private support for and interest in museums, which will generate demand for archivists, curators, and museum technicians. However, museums and other cultural institutions can be subject to cuts in funding during recessions or periods of budget tightening, reducing demand for these workers. Although the rate of turnover among archivists and curators is relatively low, the need to replace workers who leave the occupation or retire will create some additional job openings.

Salary and Compensation

Archivist, curator, conservator, and museum technician positions garner varying degrees of compensation. According to government statistics, the median annual earnings of archivists is about $36,500, with the middle 50 percent earning between $28,900 and $46,500, the lowest 10 percent earning less than $21,800, and the highest 10 percent earning more than $61,300. Median annual earnings of curators are about $43,600. The middle 50 percent of curators earn between $32,800 and $58,200, the lowest 10 percent earn less than $25,400, and the highest 10 percent earn more than $77,500. Median annual earnings of museum technicians and conservators are approximately $31,800, with the middle 50 percent earning between $23,800 and $43,000, the lowest 10 percent earning less than $18,200, and the highest 10 percent earning more than $58,300. This means that the pay isn't as substantial as in other areas in which geologists might work, even though the degree requirement is comparable. Some museums and libraries will pay for their employees to further their education if it's applicable to the field, so joining such an organization at the ground level and working while going to school might be an attractive option.

Compensation for those working for the federal government is more favorable. The average annual salary for archivists working for the federal government in nonsupervisory, supervisory, and managerial positions is about $75,800; museum curators make approximately $76,000 a year; museum specialists and technicians earn about $55,000 annually; and archives technicians can expect to receive somewhere in the region of $41,300 annually. In addition, workers employed by the federal, state, or local government tend to have good benefits and very secure jobs.

Paleogeology

Paleontology is the study of the history of life on Earth, as reflected in the fossil record. Fossils are the remains of various organisms, including plants, animals, fungi, bacteria and other single-celled living things, that are preserved in the Earth's crust and sediment. Fossils tell scientists about how animals, plants, and organisms evolve and how the climate of the Earth has changed over time. This allows scientists to make predictions about future directions of the Earth's evolution. Paleogeology is a specific aspect of paleontology that examines ancient rock and sediments.

Paleogeologists are scientists who study the physical characteristics of past geologic ages, such as the Jurassic or Triassic periods. One of the aims of paleogeologists is to be able to reconstruct past climates to understand how natural features have evolved. For example, they may examine the impact receding glaciers had on the formation of the Great Lakes. They may work with evolutionary biologists, developmental biologists, and physical anthropologists to understand the evolution of man or to collect and catalog elvenmillion-year-old fossils and the sediment surrounding them.

Paleogeologists generally divide their work between the laboratory and the field, although some may work exclusively in one area or the other. In the laboratory, paleogeologists study and identify microscopic field samples. This is time-consuming and exacting work that can be extremely satisfying for those with great attention to detail. Those specializing in field work and are often involved in geological mapping or leading field studies. Along with the excitement of leading a field excavation and obtaining ancient geological specimens, however, comes the potentially tedious work of cleaning, preparing, and analyzing specimens.

Fieldwork may; be the area most glamorized by those interested in work as a paleogeologist, however, there can be tedium and hazards in the field that are worth considering. Some hazards of fieldwork include rustic transportation to remote locations, exposure to the elements, and dehydration when working in humid or dry climates with limited access to water. Hazardous animals such as snakes, ticks, and mosquitoes can also contribute to uncomfortable working and living conditions. Finally, chipping rocks and hauling carts of sediment can present physical challenges to those working in the field.

Paleogeologists work with a variety of equipment, from the simple to the complex and high-tech. The hand lens, notebook, pencil, rock pick, and fine brushes are simple tools that have been put to use for decades and are still the staple equipment for most paleogeologists. In addition, they use GPS and GIS programs and a variety of other computer programs to analyze potential excavation sites and identify, examine, and catalog specimens.

Training and Education

A paleogeologist needs a strong background in the sciences, which should include biology and geology, mathematics, chemistry, and physics. Foreign language skills are also a benefit, not only because many fieldwork sites are located in other countries, but also because many resources are written in languages other than English. Prospective paleogeologists study field and laboratory and museum work methods, and principles. Specific courses include stratigraphy, sedimentation, mineralogy, sedimentary petrology, invertebrate paleontology, ecology, invertebrate and vertebrate zoology, paleobotany, evolutionary biology, and genetics.

Systematics and taxonomy courses form the foundation of paleontological studies. These courses focus on the principles and concepts that determine what gathered specimens and data can and cannot do to answer questions about climate change, depositional environments, rates of geologic processes, and the correlation of geologic events to reconstructing geologic history. These courses provide the fundamental knowledge necessary to pursue more specific areas of paleontology, including paleogeology.

Those seriously considering a career in paleogeology have a difficult decision to make in choosing the area in which to major. The ideal arrangement in order to best enter the field is to double-major in both biology and geology.

If this is not possible, the next best choice is to major in one and take substantial coursework in the other. In addition, a strong grounding in statistical analysis and solid computer skills are essential. The more courses and experience in these areas at the undergraduate level, the better.

College should be focused on obtaining both the necessary academic coursework and fieldwork experience. Access to such experience, however, may depend on where you live and what programs your college offers. If there are limited opportunities at your school, don't be afraid to explore summer programs or semesters abroad through other colleges, universities, associations, or organizations. It's vitally important for you to have some fieldwork experience under your belt in order to be most attractive to employers.

As with most areas in which geologists work, the minimum degree requirement for working as a paleogeologist is a master's degree. Indeed, most paleogeologists have doctoral degrees in which they complete original research in a particular specialty and often publish articles in journals. A doctoral degree is almost always necessary for any serious professional career in this field, and many universities offer graduate training in paleontology, at both the master's and Ph.D. levels. A master's degree in paleogeology usually takes between two to three years of additional college to complete, while a doctoral degree typically takes from four to six years to complete if you already have a master's degree or from six to eight years if you do not.

Some students decide to pursue a master's degree before their Ph.D., while others decide to enter a doctoral program directly after graduating with their bachelor's degree. The choice of which path to follow depends upon two main variables: your comfort with conducting research and whether or not you have developed your area of focus. Most students graduating with a geology undergraduate degree have no experience with research and haven't yet settled on a specific area of interest, making pursing a master's degree first a more beneficial means of accomplishing their career goals. More schools offer master's degrees than Ph.D.s, so shopping around for a good program is not as difficult as finding the appropriate Ph.D. program. That said, you may want to consider whether you want to attend a school that also offers a doctoral program to save you from having to switch schools after obtaining your master's degree.

Colleges and universities have various strengths and areas of focus within the field of paleontology, usually depending on the interests of individual professors. Subscribe to a journal in your area of interest and note the credentials and affiliations of the various authors of articles that most intrigue you. Make an effort to contact the professors whose work interests you directly, by letter, e-mail, or phone, and arrange to visit their departments. This not only helps you learn more about their graduate programs, but may impress them with the seriousness of your interest.

Possible Employers

Universities, museums, government geological surveys, and organizations within the petroleum industry employ paleogeologists. Most professional paleogeologists in the United States today are college and university professors. They typically work in departments of geology, where they teach general geology courses in addition to paleontology. Numerous paleogeologists work for major oil companies, helping to search for petroleum. Smaller numbers of professional paleogeologists work in museums. These individuals spend the majority of their time conducting their own research and teaching, and, on occasion, consult with other museum employees on exhibits. The fewest number of paleogeologists work for government surveys, usually in geological mapping or other applied geological problem solving.

Career Outlook

Overall, there are probably fewer jobs in paleontology in the United States than there were a few years ago, but a few good jobs still become available each year. The competition for jobs is intense with numerous applicants for each available job. Expertise, specificity, and experience are essential for success. The complex blend of specialization with flexibility is rare and valuable, so do what you can to create a resume that reflects both your education and your work experience.

Fossil fuels will provide most of our consumable energy for at least the next sixty to eighty years; thus, industrial jobs will continue to have growth potential. Biostratigraphy has been and will continue to be an integral tool in the search for and production of oil and gas, resulting in economic incentives to sustain current industrial paleontology staff and reinvigorate university training programs in stratigraphically oriented paleontology.

Paleogeologists with skills in planning and leadership can move ahead within corporate organizations, although the downside is that they often leave fieldwork behind. Additionally, paleogeologists who broaden their skills and become effective explorationists are often in demand for team assignments outside of their direct area of interest. Most, however, stay within their area of specialty where there is limited growth potential within the relatively small groups of paleogeologists. In such positions, compensation is still very good and job satisfaction can be high.

Salary and Compensation

Paleogeologists can expect a fairly modest entry-level salary of approximately $36,600, however, advancement in salary is fairly quick. The average salary of those working in this area is about $67,500. The maximum is a substantial $133,300 a year.

Salary is, of course, specific to the employer for whom you work, with some paying substantially more than others. Industrial companies tend to offer higher entry-level salaries for industrial paleogeologists; these workers may make more in the $50,000 range because this is a more technical area with a smaller supply of new graduates to fill job vacancies. As with many other fields, areas in which there are shortages of employees tend to garner higher wages for the work.

Additional Job Titles

There are many subdivisions of the field of paleontology in which to work. For example, you might consider studying vertebrate paleontology (the study of fossils of animals with backbones); invertebrate paleontology (the study of fossils of animals without backbones); micropaleontology (the study of fossils of single-celled organisms); paleobotany (the study of plant fossils); taphonomy (the study of how fossils form and are preserved); biostratigraphy (the study of the vertical distribution of fossils in rocks); and paleoecology (the study of ancient ecosystems and how they developed).

For those interested in working in a geologically based museum, you may choose to work as a docent (conduct tours and guide individuals and groups through the exhibits); exhibit designer (work from themes developed by the curator to present the contents of an exhibition to the public); development officer (raise money from private sources to support the museum's activities and projects); publications' editor or writer (produce various printed material, including exhibit labels, brochures, and catalogs, and manage website content); and registrar (responsible for organizing and maintaining the records of the objects or specimens in a collection).

10

Path 5: Careers in Academia

Teaching is the career path of choice for many people who feel that their love of geology is best expressed by sharing it with others. The term "teacher" is often applied to professionals in elementary, middle, and high school settings, although those filling the top posts at colleges and universities are all, to some extent, teachers. To students, the distinctions between a high school science teacher and a university professor aren't of critical importance; despite the subject area, rank, or setting, the teaching role essentially remains the same. This chapter focuses on teaching in higher education, since that is where a geologist's specific knowledge base is most often applied.

The field of education has seen many changes over the past twenty years. Classes are less structured than in the past, with students often working in groups to discuss and solve problems together. Preparing students for the future workforce, which necessitates working as a team, is the major stimulus generating the changes in education. To be prepared, students must be able to interact with others, adapt to new technology, and logically think through problems. Teachers provide the tools and environment for their students to develop these skills.

The role of the teacher has also changed in recent years from that of a lecturer or presenter to one of a facilitator or coach. Interactive discussions and student-led learning have replaced rote memorization at all levels of education, from elementary school to colleges and universities. For example, rather than merely telling students about environmental geology, a teacher might ask students to perform a laboratory experiment, take a field trip to collect samples, or conduct a survey of their own choice and then discuss how the results apply to the real world.

Geology Teacher or Professor

Geologists in educational settings divide their time between teaching students in classroom and field settings and conducting research. Much of a professor's time is spent preparing for classes, writing lectures, grading papers, assessing student performance, working with individual students, and attending departmental meetings. Faculty members may write grant proposals, research special-interest topics, compose scholarly articles on their findings, and write longer monographs and books for the general public or textbooks for students. They may lecture to several hundred students in large halls, lead small seminars, and supervise students in laboratories. In addition, university faculty may be responsible for advising both undergraduate and graduate students, helping them define and carry out their research, and evaluating their results.

Most college and university faculty are in four academic ranks: professor, associate professor, assistant professor, and instructor. A small number are lecturers. Most faculty members are hired as instructors or assistant professors. Four-year colleges and universities generally hire people with doctoral degrees for full-time, tenure-track positions, but may hire master's degree holders or doctoral candidates for certain disciplines or for part-time and temporary jobs.

Graduate teaching assistants, often referred to as graduate TAs, assist faculty, department chairs, or other professional staff at colleges and universities by performing teaching or teaching-related duties. In addition to their work responsibilities, assistants have their own school commitments, as they are also students who are working towards earning a graduate degree, such as a Ph.D. Some teaching assistants have full responsibility for teaching a course—usually one that is introductory in nature—which can include preparation of lectures and exams, and assigning final grades to students. Others provide assistance to faculty members, which may consist of a variety of tasks such as grading papers, monitoring exams, holding office hours or help-sessions for students, conducting laboratory sessions, or administering quizzes to the class. This type of work can be stressful, particularly when assistants are given full responsibility for teaching a class; however, this position allows graduate students the opportunity to gain valuable teaching experience, which is especially helpful for those seeking to become faculty members at colleges and universities after completing their degree.

Possible Employers

Postsecondary professors teach and advise over sixteen million full-time and part-time college students at community colleges, state universities, and private colleges. These institutions can be very large, small, or somewhere in between.

Private colleges may have a particular foundation on which all curricula is built, such as a service- or religious-based foundation. State universities may be large organizations with a significant science department, which means the professor must be adept at navigating institutional politics. In essence, every institution of higher education has its own personality, so understanding your likes and dislikes and conducting research about the educational environment before accepting the job is vitally important.

Most faculty members serve on academic, administrative, or research committees that deal with the policies of their institution, departmental matters, academic issues, curricula, budgets, equipment purchases, and hiring. Some professors also work with student organizations. The amount of time spent on each of these activities varies by individual circumstance and type of institution. For example, faculty members at universities generally spend a significant part of their time conducting research; those in four-year colleges, somewhat less; and those in two-year colleges, relatively little. Despite this, however, the teaching load is usually heavier in two-year colleges.

University faculty jobs differ from those at community colleges. The main area of difference is the degree to which they emphasize research versus writing. Colleges and universities tend to emphasize the quality and caliber of faculty scholarship through research and writing more than the teaching process. In geology this usually takes the form of producing books, although the pressure to produce published works varies by institution. Community colleges, on the other hand, tend to focus more on the course content and the professor's teaching skills. Another difference is that four-year university or college faculty teach introductory- and upper-level undergraduate courses, or they may concentrate solely on graduate courses, whereas community college faculty teach mostly introductory-level courses leading to an associate's degree.

College and university faculty are organized into departments or divisions based on subject or field. Geologists may work in a geology department, for example, or in a chemistry or engineering department. They usually teach several different courses in their department: introduction to geology, hydrogeology, engineering geology, land use planning, or groundwater geophysics, for example. Department heads generally have heavier administrative responsibilities and spend less time in the classroom.

Some college professors are hired as consultants by government, businesses, and nonprofit and community organizations. Federal and state governments work with college and university faculty most significantly in conducting national research projects. Since funding for these types of projects often depends on the availability of grants and contracts, those typically hired generally have a proven ability to secure funding from an external source.

Training and Education

No matter what the subfield of geological education—mining, the oil and gas industry, environmental, or the many other geosciences—there are qualities and skills that all educators most possess. In addition to being knowledgeable in their subject, having the ability to communicate, inspire trust and confidence, and motivate students, and to understand their educational and emotional needs, is essential for teachers. They also should be organized, dependable, and patient, as well as creative. Teaching requires a wide variety of skills and aptitudes, including a talent for working with people; organizational, administrative, and record-keeping abilities; research and communication skills; the power to influence, motivate, and train others; patience; and creativity.

The nature of the degree you must possess in order to get a job varies depending on the type of educational institution for which you would like to work. To work in most elementary, intermediate, or high school systems teaching science courses, a bachelor's degree with a teaching certification is required. Community colleges require teachers to hold master's degrees and sometimes Ph.D.s, whereas colleges and universities require applicants to possess doctoral degrees. Preference is usually given to candidates with previous teaching and/or research experience. Research activities of the successful candidate should complement existing programs, such as petrology, geochronology, and stratigraphy. In addition, areas of specialty are more often considered in higher educational settings. Field-oriented bedrock geology may be a priority within a particular department of geological sciences, and preference may be given to a field-oriented structural geologist with such specialized interests as those in tectonics and sedimentation, plate kinematics, and northern Appalachian geology.

Doctoral programs take an average of six years of full-time study beyond the bachelor's degree, including time spent completing a master's degree and a dissertation. Some programs, such as those in the humanities, may take longer to complete; others, such as those in engineering, usually are shorter. Candidates specialize in a subfield of a discipline, but also take courses covering the entire discipline. Programs typically include twenty or more increasingly specialized courses and seminars plus comprehensive examinations on all major areas of the field. Candidates also must complete a dissertation— a written report on original research in the candidate's major field of study that usually takes one or two years of full-time work. The dissertation sets forth an original hypothesis or proposes a model and tests it, and it is researched and written under the guidance of one or more faculty advisors.

When choosing a doctoral program, make sure it encourages close communication with faculty. Choose your dissertation committee carefully and develop a good working relationship with your adviser. Make sure the members of your committee are compatible with you and share an interest in your work. They should be generous with their time and well funded in their own work. You always need to think in terms of fundable research, so pick an area that is being funded by the U.S. government or other entities. Also find out whether faculty members regularly coauthor articles with students, which can help you to publish your research.

To qualify for a position as a graduate teaching assistant, candidates must be enrolled in a graduate school program. In addition, some colleges and universities require teaching assistants to attend classes or take some training prior to being given responsibility for a course. Although graduate teaching assistants usually work at the institution and in the department where they are earning their degree, teaching or internship positions for graduate students at institutions that do not grant a graduate degree have become more common in recent years. For example, a program called Preparing Future Faculty (preparing-faculty.org), administered by the Association of American Colleges and Universities (aacu-edu.org) and the Council of Graduate Schools (cgsnet.org), has led to the creation of many now-independent programs that offer graduate students at research universities the opportunity to work as teaching assistants at other types of institutions, such as liberal arts or community colleges. These programs provide valuable learning opportunities for graduate students interested in teaching at the postsecondary level, and also help to make these students aware of the differences among the various types of institutions at which they may someday work.

Teachers of junior and high school grades either major in geology as the subject they plan to teach while also taking education courses, or major in education and take geology or other earth science courses as their subject. For those geologists who choose teaching these grades after having already gained a bachelor's degree in geology, many states offer alternative teacher certification programs for people who have college training in the subject they will teach, but do not have the necessary education courses required for a regular certificate. Aspiring teachers who need certification may also enter programs that grant a master's degree in education, as well as certification. States also issue emergency certificates to individuals who do not meet all requirements for a regular certificate when schools cannot hire enough teachers with regular certificates.

Almost all states require applicants for teacher certification to be tested for competency in basic skills such as reading and writing, teaching skills, or subject matter proficiency. Almost all require continuing education for renewal of the teacher's certificate, and some require a master's degree. Many states have reciprocity agreements that make it easier for teachers certified in one state to become certified in another. Teachers may become board-certified by successfully completing the National Board for Professional Teaching Standards certification process. This certification is voluntary, but may result in a higher salary. Information on certification requirements and approved teacher training institutions is available from local school systems and state departments of education.

With additional preparation and certification, teachers may become administrators or supervisors, although the number of positions is limited. In some systems, highly qualified, experienced teachers can become senior or mentor teachers, with higher pay and additional responsibilities. They guide and assist less experienced teachers while keeping most of their teaching responsibilities.

Some faculty, based on teaching experience, research, publication, and service on campus committees and task forces move into administrative and managerial positions, such as departmental chairperson, dean, and president. At four-year institutions, such advancement requires a doctoral degree.

Career Outlook

According to the Bureau of Labor Statistics, the overall employment of teachers is expected to increase faster than the average for all occupations through 2014, although many of these will be part-time positions. While projected employment growth varies among individual teaching occupations, job openings for all teachers are expected to increase substantially as increasing numbers of teachers now in their fifties reach retirement age.

Opportunities for those working in education vary depending on the position. For those holding a master's degree, job prospects in the near future are expected to be favorable, as community colleges and other institutions that employ them, such as professional career education programs, are expected to experience considerable growth. Opportunities for graduate teaching assistants are expected to be very good due to much higher undergraduate enrollments coupled with more modest graduate enrollment increases. Constituting almost 9 percent of all postsecondary teachers, graduate teaching assistants play an integral role in the postsecondary education system, and they are expected to continue to do so in the future. One of the main reasons why students attend postsecondary institutions is to prepare themselves for careers, so the best job prospects for postsecondary teachers are likely to be in fields where job growth is expected to be strong over the next decade. These include jobs teaching aspects of environmental and mining and petroleum geology.

The most coveted jobs at universities are those that lead to tenure. Tenure track positions are stable ones because the professor cannot be fired or let go from his or her position. In order to obtain this level of security, however, the person has to prove the quality of his or her teaching and scholarship before being granted tenure; this usually takes from five to seven years.

Before getting tenure, a faculty member usually has to work very hard, proving that he or she can produce scholarship of a quality that gets published in the most prestigious journals. One's peers often appreciate innovative and creative ideas, but these characteristics may not be recognized in the tenure-granting process. In order to ensure tenure, one must be willing to work within what may be a bureaucratic structure of the college or university and one must be a top-grade teacher who consistently scores high with students and faculty alike.

After being granted tenure, faculty members may concentrate on conducting new research, setting up academic programs, supervising student research, writing books or articles for publication, or teaching. There is a great opportunity to know students and help them mature personally and intellectually. Many faculty find great rewards in this. Before committing to this line of work, you should ask yourself if you are willing to put up with many years of graduate education, years of fieldwork, and then frequent job hunting with no guarantee of a tenured teaching or research position.

The number of tenure-track positions has declined in recent years as institutions seek flexibility in dealing with financial matters and changing student interests. Today, institutions rely more heavily on limited term contracts and part-time, or adjunct, faculty, thus shrinking the total pool of tenured faculty. Limited-term contracts—typically two to five years, may be terminated or extended when they expire, but generally do not lead to tenure. In addition, some institutions have limited the percentage of faculty who can be tenured.

Salary and Compensation

The salaries of teachers in junior and high school settings vary. According to the Bureau of Labor Statistics, the median average salary of teachers of grades six through high school range from $41,400 to $45,920; the lowest 10 percent earn $26,730 to $31,180; and the top 10 percent earn $66,240 to $71,370. According to the American Federation of Teachers (aft.org), beginning teachers with a bachelor's degree earn an average of $31,704. Private school teachers generally earn less than public school teachers, but may be given other benefits, such as free or subsidized housing. Finally, more than half of all elementary, middle, and secondary school teachers belong to unions—mainly the American Federation of Teachers and the National Education Association (nea.org)—that bargain with school systems over wages, hours, and other terms and conditions of employment.

Teachers can boost their salary in a number of ways. In some schools, teachers receive extra pay for coaching sports and working with students in extracurricular activities. Getting a master's degree or national certification often results in a raise in pay, as does acting as a mentor. Some teachers earn extra income during the summer by teaching summer school or performing other jobs in the school system.

Earnings for those teaching in institutions of higher education also vary according to faculty rank and type of institution, geographic area, and field. Median annual earnings of all postsecondary teachers are about $51,800. The middle 50 percent earn between $36,590 and $72,490; the lowest 10 percent earn less than $25,460; and the highest 10 percent earn more than $99,980. According to a 2004–2005 survey by the American Association of University Professors, salaries for full-time faculty averaged $68,505. By rank, the average was $91,548 for professors, $65,113 for associate professors, $54,571 for assistant professors, $39,899 for instructors, and $45,647 for lecturers. Faculties in four-year colleges or universities earn higher salaries, on average, than do those in community colleges. For example, faculty salaries average $79,342 in private independent institutions, $66,851 in public institutions, and $61,103 in religiously affiliated private colleges and universities. The starting salary range for community college teachers ranges from $31,947 to $38,611, depending upon degrees and experience.

Many faculty members have significant earnings in addition to their base salary, from consulting, teaching additional courses, research, writing for publication, or other employment. In addition, many college and university faculty enjoy some unique benefits, including access to campus facilities, tuition waivers for dependents, housing and travel allowances, and paid sabbaticals; part-time faculty usually have fewer benefits than full-time faculty, however.

Many geologists find teaching to be a rewarding career choice filled with lifelong learning and the ability to show others the wonders of the field. If you are a people person and you love learning new things every day, then you should seriously consider becoming a teacher. Start out by working as a teaching assistant in graduate school or become a classroom assistant to a middle or high school science teacher so you can get a better feel for working with various age groups. No matter whom you decide to teach, you're sure to have fulfilling career!

APPENDIX A

Professional Associations

Academy of Certified Archivists
certifiedarchivists.org

American Association of Museums
aam-us.org

American Association of Petroleum Geologists
aapg.org

American Association of University Professors
aaup.org

American Federation of Teachers
aft.org

American Geological Institute
agiweb.org

American Geophysical Union
agu.org

American Institute of Hydrology
aihydro.org

American Institute of Mining, Metallurgical, and Petroleum Engineers
aimeny.org

American Society of Civil Engineers
asce.org

Association of Science-Technology Centers
awg.org

Association of American Colleges and Universities
aacu-edu.org

Association of Earth Science Editors
aese.org

Association of Science-Technology Centers
astc.org

Chronicle of Higher Education
http://chronicle.com

Council of Graduate Schools
cgsnet.org

Geological Society of America
geosociety.org

International Association of Geomorphologists
geomorph.org

International Association of Sedimentologists
iasnet.org

Marine Technology Society
mtsociety.org

Mineralogical Society of America
minsocam.org

National Academy of Sciences
nationalacademies.org

National Association of Colleges and Employers
naceweb.org

National Board for Professional Teaching Standards
nbpts.org

National Council for Accreditation of Teacher Education
ncate.org

National Education Association
nea.org

National Oceanic and Atmospheric Administration
U.S. Department of Commerce
noaa.gov

Paleontological Research Institution
priweb.org

Paleontological Society
paleosoc.org

Smithsonian Institution
si.edu

Society of Exploration Geophysicists
seg.org

Society for Mining, Metallurgy, and Exploration, Inc.
smenet.org

Society of Petroleum Engineers
spe.org

Society of Vertebrate Paleontology
vertpaleo.org

U.S. Department of Defense
defenselink.mil

U.S. Department of the Interior
doi.gov

U.S. Geological Survey
usgs.gov

APPENDIX B

Geology Career Websites

CareerBuilder
careerbuilder.com

CareerMine
infomine.com/careers/positions/

CareerMosaic
recruitmentresources.com/careermosaic.html

Careers in the Geosciences
agiweb.org/career/

Earth Science World
earthscienceworld.org

Earthworks
earthworks-jobs.com

Geologist Jobs
http://geology.com/jobs.htm

Geotimes
geotimes.org/current/index.html

HigherCareers
highercareers.com

Hire Rocket
ggrweb.com/job.html

InfoMine
infomine.com

JobHunt
job-hunt.org

Monster
monster.com

Outdoor Action Guide to Outdoor/Environmental Careers
princeton.edu/~oa/jobs/careeroe.html

Preparing Future Faculty
preparing-faculty.org

U.S. Geological Survey Online Automated Recruitment System
usgs.gov/ohr/oars

U.S.G.S. Coastal and Marine Geology Program
http://marine.usgs.gov

World Wide Worker
worldwideworker.com

Index

About the Author

A full-time writer of career books, Blythe Camenson wants to help job seekers make educated choices. She believes that, with enough information, readers can find long-term, satisfying careers. To that end, she researches traditional as well as unusual occupations, providing readers with a bevy of information, from educational requirements to earnings.

Camenson was educated in Boston, earning her B.A. in English and psychology from the University of Massachusetts and her M.Ed. in counseling from Northeastern University.

This edition of *Great Jobs for Geology Majors* was revised by a freelance writer specializing in career search topics.